Dedication

To Becky Dutcher, my friend and soul sister.
Thank you for always being there for me.

This Book Is Safari Enabled

The Safari® Enabled icon on the cover of your favorite technology book means the book is available through Safari Bookshelf. When you buy this book, you get free access to the online edition for 45 days.

Safari Bookshelf is an electronic reference library that lets you easily search thousands of technical books, find code samples, download chapters, and access technical information whenever and wherever you need it.

To gain 45-day Safari Enabled access to this book:

• Go to **http://www.peachpit.com/safarienabled**

• Complete the brief registration form

• Enter the coupon code 2VOQ-WYSN-WQJR-PQN7-3CYO

If you have difficulty registering on Safari Bookshelf or accessing the online edition, please e-mail customer-service@safaribooksonline.com.

Acknowledgments

Even though this book has my name all over it, many people helped in getting it from paper to press.

Most importantly I'd like to thank Ted Alspach. His confidence and encouragement guide me through all that I do. He is truly my inspiration.

Many thank you's to Gage and Dakota who put up with my rantings and ravings as I was finishing up this book. They learned my mantra "Just one more chapter."

Thanks go out to my mom and dad who always encouraged me to do the best I can do and still be happy.

I'll always be thankful to my support group of friends: Becky Dutcher, Tracey Shobert, Christie Brown, and Melanie Rejebian. They are the best group of friends anyone could have!

The Acrobat team at Adobe, which has revolutionized the way that documents are distributed around the world.

Becky Morgan and Nancy Peterson, my editors at Peachpit Press. They took these words and ideas and helped mold them into a wonderful, informative piece of work.

Thanks to Lisa Brazieal for making this major update look so good. And to Liz Welch, copyeditor, who made some brilliant catches.

Many thanks to John Deubert, technical editor, who went above and beyond the call of duty.

Last but not least, thanks to everyone at Peachpit Press who helped move this book along and get it into your hands.

VISUAL QUICKSTART GUIDE

ADOBE ACROBAT 7

FOR WINDOWS AND MACINTOSH

Jennifer Alspach

Peachpit Press

Visual QuickStart Guide
Adobe Acrobat 7 for Windows and Macintosh
Jennifer Alspach

Peachpit Press
1249 Eighth Street
Berkeley, CA 94710
510/524-2178
800/283-9444
510/524-2221 (fax)
Find us on the World Wide Web at: www.peachpit.com
To report errors, please send a note to errata@peachpit.com
Peachpit Press is a division of Pearson Education

Copyright © 2005 by Jennifer Alspach

Project Editor: Becky Morgan
Editor: Nancy Peterson
Production Editor: Lisa Brazieal
Copyeditor: Liz Welch
Technical Editor: John Deubert
Compositor: Sean McDonald
Indexer: Julie Bess
Cover design: The Visual Group
Cover Production: George Mattingly

Notice of rights

Notice of liability
The information in this book is distributed on an "As Is" basis, without warranty. While every precaution has been taken in the preparation of the book, neither the author nor Peachpit shall have any liability to any person or entity with respect to any loss or damage caused or alleged to be caused directly or indirectly by the instructions contained in this book or by the computer software and hardware products described in it.

Trademarks
Visual QuickStart Guide is a registered trademark of Peachpit, a division of Pearson Education.
Adobe, Acrobat, the Acrobat logo, Acrobat Capture, Adobe Reader, Illustrator, Photoshop, and PostScript are either registered trademarks or trademarks of Adobe Systems Incorporated in the United States and/or other countries. All other trademarks are the property of their respective owners.
Throughout this book, trademarks are used. Rather than put a trademark symbol in every occurrence of a trademarked name, we state that we are using the names in an editorial fashion only and to the benefit of the trademark owner with no intention of infringement of the trademark.

ISBN 0-321-30331-8

9 8 7 6 5 4 3 2 1

Printed and bound in the United States of America

TABLE OF CONTENTS

TABLE OF CONTENTS

ACROBAT BASICS

Adobe Acrobat's Portable Document Format (PDF) is truly amazing. This file format lets you read any electronic document on almost any computer system. Anyone with the free Adobe Reader software can open and view a document converted to a PDF, and it will look exactly the way it did in the original authoring program (such as Microsoft Word or Adobe InDesign). It doesn't matter how the document was originally created.

Acrobat lets you do more than just read a PDF file; you can also edit its text, add pages, include comments, start a review, create a form for the Web, add links, create navigational structures, and even turn a PDF into a multimedia presentation with dazzling transitions between pages. I'll deal with the more complex features in later chapters. For now, let's look at the basic features to get a general idea of what this software can do for you.

Starting and Quitting Acrobat

Starting Acrobat is no different from starting any other Windows or Mac program.

To run Acrobat:

◆ Locate the Acrobat icon and double-click it (**Figure 1.1**).

Acrobat will load and become the active program.

To quit Acrobat:

◆ Choose Exit (Windows)/Quit (Mac) from the File/Acrobat menu (Ctrl+Q/Command+Q).

Any open Acrobat documents close automatically. If you made changes to a document, a dialog box appears, asking whether you want to save those changes.

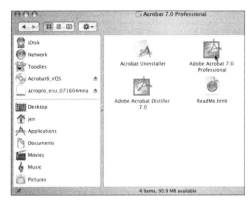

Figure 1.1 Double-click on the Acrobat icon to launch the application.

Navigation Pane *Document Pane*

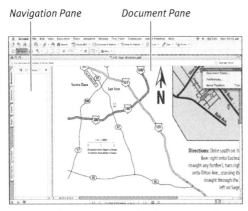

Figure 1.2 The Document window has 2 panes: the Navigation pane and the Document pane.

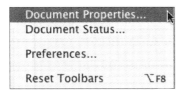

Figure 1.3 The quick access window lets you get detailed information on the document.

Understanding the Acrobat Screen

Acrobat has a modular, customizable interface. Most of the tools and panes you see on the screen can be separated from their neighbors, moved to different parts of the screen, combined in groups as you see fit, or banished altogether.

Running across the top of the application window is the menu bar, containing the pull-down menus. Just below the menu bar are the toolbars, which give you quick access to the most commonly used commands for file manipulation, viewing, and navigation.

The document window is divided into two panes (**Figure 1.2**). The Navigation pane, along the left-hand side of the window, provides sophisticated controls for finding your way through a PDF document. Most of the screen is occupied by the Document pane, which contains the file itself. Clicking on the small right-pointing arrow in the upper-right corner of the Document pane brings up a menu (**Figure 1.3**) that provides quick access to detailed information about your document, as well as the Preferences dialog box. The status bar along the bottom of the document window (**Figure 1.4**) offers alternative methods for displaying your document, such as one or two pages at a time.

First page *Page number* *Last page*

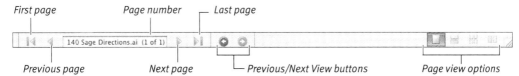

Previous page *Next page* *Previous/Next View buttons* *Page view options*

Figure 1.4 Along the bottom of the pane is the status bar.

Finally, there are six panes—Bookmarks, Signatures, Layers, Pages, Attachments, and Comments (**Figure 1.5**)—that are probably the most flexible elements of the Acrobat interface. Each pane has its own pop-up menu of options, and can be pulled out of the Navigation pane and placed anywhere on the screen.

An additional pane you can show on startup is the How To pane (a pane that presents step-by-step instructions for certain common tasks, such as adding a watermark or creating PDF files from image files). If you want the pane to be visible on startup, choose Help > How To > Show at Startup. For more on the How To pane, see Appendix A.

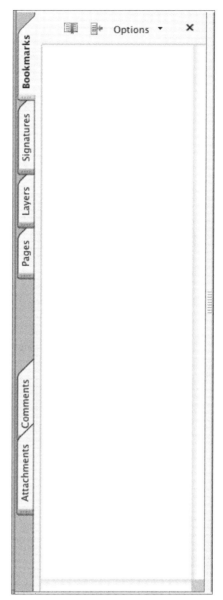

Figure 1.5 A quick way to get to many of the features in Acrobat is through the Navigation panes.

Using the Toolbars

What appears to be a single toolbar is actually a collection of toolbars—File, Tasks, Basic, Zoom, Rotate, and Help—that you can hide or show as you desire (**Figure 1.6**).

The toolbars (**Figures 1.7** through **1.12**) are pretty easy to use: Simply click the button for the tool you want to use. To send a file to the printer, for instance, just click the Print button and the Print dialog box opens. Some buttons are hiding multiple tools, which are revealed when you click the top-level, visible button.

Figure 1.6 Show or hide the collection of toolbars under the menus.

Figure 1.7. Go to the File toolbar for quick file management.

Figure 1.8 The Tasks toolbar is for marking up and commenting on documents.

Figure 1.9 The tools on the Basic toolbar let you change and add to documents.

Hand tool   Snapshot tool

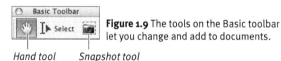

Figure 1.10 The tools on the Zoom toolbar let you increase or decrease magnification of the document.

Figure 1.11 The Rotate toolbar does exactly what its name promises.

Figure 1.12 The Help toolbar gives you quick access to the Help functions.

✔ Tips

- If you don't like the way the toolbars are arranged, change 'em around! Position the pointer over the vertical separator bar on the left side of the toolbar you want to move, then drag the toolbar to its new position. Any toolbars in the way of the one you've moved will step politely out of the way to accommodate the newcomer.

- Although you can move toolbars around the screen, you can't change their shape or orientation.

- Can't remember what a particular toolbar button does? Thanks to the magic of tool tips, any button will tell you its name—just let the pointer hover over it for a second or two (**Figure 1.13**).

To hide and show individual toolbars:

1. To see a list of toolbars, do one of the following:

   ▲ Choose Toolbars from the View menu.

   A submenu pops out, showing a list of all of the available toolbars (**Figure 1.14**).

   ▲ Right-click (Windows) or Control-click (Mac) any individual toolbar.

   A contextual menu will appear, listing all of the toolbars.

   Whether you work with the contextual menu or the submenu, the currently visible toolbars have a checkmark by their names.

2. To hide a toolbar that is showing, click its name in the Toolbars menu so the checkmark disappears. To display a hidden toolbar, click its name so the checkmark appears.

Figure 1.13 A tool tip pops up to identify the object your mouse is hovering over.

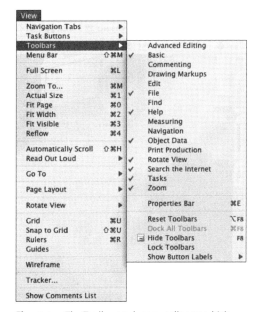

Figure 1.14 The Toolbars submenu tells you which toolbars are visible.

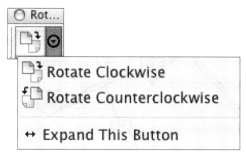

Figure 1.15 More tools are hiding beneath the arrow in the toolbars.

Figure 1.16 Choose Expand This Button and guess what happens.

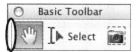

Figure 1.17 Drag and hold the vertical line to the left of the tools to move a toolbar off the main bar.

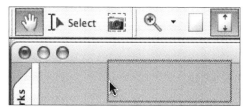

Figure 1.18 Move any toolbar anywhere on your screen.

✔ Tip

- Press F8 to quickly show or hide all of the toolbars at once.

Some toolbars keep a few command buttons tucked away out of sight. The key to unlocking these secret commands is the More Tools feature, marked by a minuscule downward-pointing arrow to the right of certain toolbar buttons (**Figure 1.15**).

To display and re-hide hidden toolbar buttons:

1. Click a More Tools button to see a menu of that toolbar's hidden commands. Choose an item from the menu to activate the command.

2. Choose Expand This Button at the bottom of the More Tools menu to add the hidden buttons to the toolbar (**Figure 1.16**). The More Tools button transforms into the Collapse button, marked by a left-pointing arrow, to indicate that the button has been expanded.

3. To tuck away a toolbar's expanded buttons, click its Collapse button. The toolbar returns to its default state.

Rearranging toolbars

A really cool feature of Acrobat is the ability to move your toolbars. You can put the tools you access regularly in a more convenient spot. You can rearrange a toolbar's order in the main toolbar, and make a separate floating toolbar anywhere on your screen. To separate a toolbar or turn it into a floating toolbar, click on the vertical bar beside a tool and drag it anywhere on your screen (**Figure 1.17** and **Figure 1.18**).

USING THE TOOLBARS

About the Menus

Acrobat's pull-down menus—File, Edit, View, Document, Tools, Advanced, Window, Comments, and Help—are in the menu bar running along the top of the application window. On the Macintosh, there is an additional menu called Acrobat (**Figure 1.19**). To access a menu's commands, simply click the menu, then choose the menu item you want.

✔ Tip

- Press Ctrl+Shift+M (Windows)/ Command+Shift+M (Mac) to show or hide the menu bar.

Figure 1.19 Mac users have an additional menu: the Acrobat menu.

Figure 1.20 The Document menu holds commands for commenting on and signing documents.

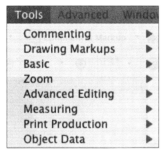

Figure 1.21 The Tools menu lets you get to important tools, like drawing, editing, and Object Data tools.

Acrobat's Menus

◆ The **File** menu handles basic file operations such as opening, closing, creating and printing PDFs, and setting document-specific parameters.

◆ The **Edit** menu provides basic search tools and editing commands, including Copy, Cut, Paste, and Check Spelling.

◆ The **View** menu allows you to adjust how Acrobat displays the document: its magnification and orientation, or the number of pages. You can also show or hide panes and toolbars from this menu.

◆ The **Document** menu (**Figure 1.20**) allows you to comment on, attach files to, and digitally sign a PDF, and add headers, footers, watermarks, backgrounds, and pages. Use the tools in this menu to add, import, and export comments.

◆ The **Tools** menu (**Figure 1.21**) contains industrial-strength commands for operations such as commenting, processing, viewing, and editing.

(continues on next page)

ABOUT THE MENUS

◆ The **Advanced** menu (**Figure 1.21**) provides commands for using Acrobat Distiller (which lets you convert PostScript files to PDFs), forms, and for exporting images. This is where you'll also find the submenus Accessibility, Digital Editions (for downloading and reading eBooks), JavaScript (a programming language built into Acrobat), and Web Capture (used for converting Web sites to PDFs).

◆ The **Window** menu's commands let you customize your workspace. You can choose not only which document window is in the foreground, but also how Acrobat arranges multiple documents.

◆ The **Comments** menu's commands (**Figure 1.22**) includes commands for adding comments and creating a review process.

◆ In the **Help** menu you'll find assistance, including access to Acrobat Help and Adobe's Web-based support. The How To feature, which opens a special pane, takes you step by step through many types of task.

Figure 1.22 The Advanced menu gives you access to advanced areas, such as Accessibility, Digital IDs, JavaScript, and Batch processing.

Figure 1.23 The Comments menu allows you to add comments and send documents for review.

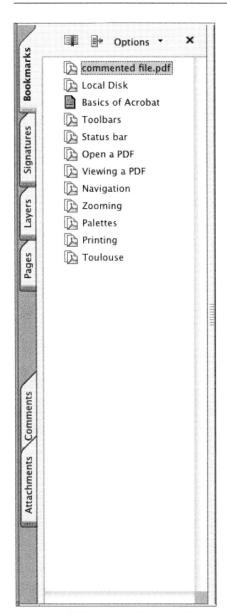

Figure 1.24 Click a bookmark in the Bookmarks pane to jump to its specified location.

Exploring Acrobat's Panes

The panes are mini-windows that assist you in finding your way through a PDF document—Bookmarks, Signatures, Layers, Pages, Attachments, and Comments. By default, the panes are "docked" in the Navigation pane of the document window, but the panes can be moved, resized, and grouped. When they're in the Navigation pane, you can see the tabs of all panes (which is why Adobe refers to them as "tabbed panes"), but only the top pane's contents are visible. Just click a tab to see the contents of another pane.

You can pull a tabbed pane out of the Navigation pane by clicking its tab and dragging it anywhere on the screen. Then it's called a "floating panel," and you can move it freely around the screen by dragging its label. You can also group floating panels together by dragging the tab of one into the window of another.

◆ The **Bookmarks** pane displays the bookmarks added to the PDF by the document's author (**Figure 1.24**). Click a bookmark to jump to that point in the document. You can create and edit bookmarks as well. For more information, see Chapter 6.

(continues on next page)

EXPLORING ACROBAT'S PANES

◆ The **Signatures** pane shows any digital signatures that have been added to the document. This pane also displays information about the digital signature (**Figure 1.25**). Learn more about digital signatures in Chapter 14.

◆ The **Layers** pane displays any layers that were transferred from the authoring application. You can examine a layer and show or hide its contents (**Figure 1.26**).

Figure 1.25 This window shows information about who has digitally signed the document and whether it has been altered since it was signed.

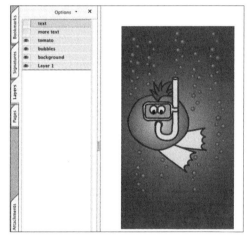

Figure 1.26 Show and hide different layers with the Layers pane.

EXPLORING ACROBAT'S PANES

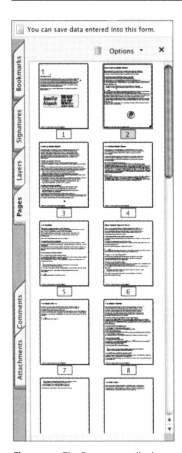

Figure 1.27 The Pages pane displays thumbnail views of each page in the document.

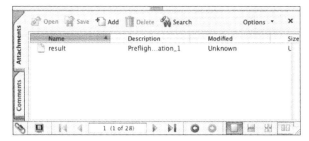

Figure 1.28 The Attachment pane displays icons showing the attachments added to a PDF document.

◆ The **Pages** pane displays a small image, or thumbnail, of each page of the document (**Figure 1.27**). You can move to a page quickly by clicking its thumbnail. You can add or delete pages, or change the order of pages in a document, just by dragging their thumbnails around. Thumbnails are discussed in more detail in Chapter 5.

◆ The **Attachment** pane displays any attachments added to the PDF document (**Figure 1.28**).

(continues on next page)

EXPLORING ACROBAT'S PANES

◆ The **Comments** pane displays a list of the comments that have been added to a document (**Figure 1.29**). For more information on comments, see Chapter 7.

Acrobat has several other panes as well, which you can access through the View > Navigation Tabs submenu.

◆ The **Articles** pane lists the articles that a document's author *defines*, or selects (**Figure 1.30**). (An *article* identifies separate blocks of text as a single story, similar to a newspaper article that may start on page 1 and then continue on page 13.) Double-click an article to read it from the beginning. Articles are discussed in more detail in Chapter 6.

◆ The **Destinations** pane shows destinations (named link targets) that have been established in the document (**Figure 1.31**). Double-click a destination to jump to that spot in the document.

◆ The **Content** pane (**Figure 1.32**) displays the name of the PDF and the number of pages in the document.

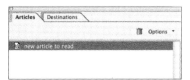

Figure 1.29 The Comments pane displays all the comments appended to the document.

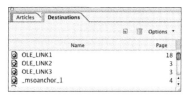

Figure 1.30 The Articles pane lists any articles defined in the document.

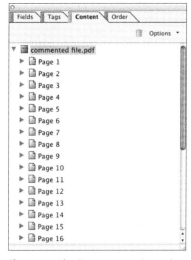

Figure 1.31 The Destinations pane shows links that have been set up between documents.

Figure 1.32 The Content pane shows the name of the PDF and the number of pages.

EXPLORING ACROBAT'S PANES

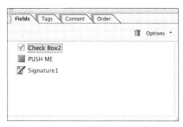

Figure 1.33 The Fields pane shows the fields defined in the PDF.

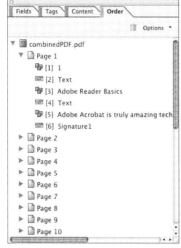

Figure 1.34 The Order pane shows the pages in full detail, from text to text fields and signatures.

Figure 1.35 The Tags pane shows you the tagged areas of the PDF in the order it was tagged.

◆ The **Fields** pane (**Figure 1.33**) displays the fields (interactive controls, such as a check box or a name field, for collecting information in a form) in the document and lists them by the order in which they appear.

◆ The **Order** pane (**Figure 1.34**) displays the pages in detail. In the Order pane, you can see everything that is on one page at a time, including the text, text fields, and signatures. Use this to change the order of the specific sections of each page.

◆ The **Tags** pane (**Figure 1.35**) shows each tagged area of the PDF in the order in which it was tagged originally. A tag identifies objects, text, and other elements in a PDF document.

(continues on next page)

EXPLORING ACROBAT'S PANES

◆ The **Info** pane shows you the position of the pointer relative to the top-left corner of the document (**Figure 1.36**). If you're making a selection (for example, selecting text or graphics, or defining a form field), the pane also shows the dimensions of that selection. You can change the unit of measurement—points, inches, or millimeters—from the Info pane's menu.

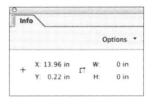

Figure 1.36 The Info pane shows you the position of the pointer relative to the top-left corner of the document.

To show or hide the Navigation pane:

1. If the Navigation pane is hidden, choose View > Navigation Tabs > Show Navigation Pane, or press F4.

2. To hide the open the Navigation pane, choose View > Navigation Tabs > Hide Navigation Pane, or press F4.

✔ Tips

■ You can also click on one of the tabs on the left to show the pane. Click on the tab again to hide the pane.

■ Don't confuse the Navigation pane with the Navigation tools in the status bar at the bottom of the Document pane. Those can't be removed or hidden. (See the following section for more about the status bar.)

To show or hide a pane:

1. To show a pane, choose it from the Navigation Tabs submenu of the View menu. A checkmark will appear next to its name and it will become visible.

2. To hide a tabbed pane, choose it from the Navigation Tabs submenu of the View menu. The checkmark will disappear from its name and only the tab will be visible.

    or

    To hide a floating pane, click the close button in the upper-right corner (upper-left corner for Macs) of its window (**Figure 1.37**).

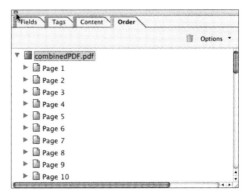

Figure 1.37 Click the close button in the upper-right (Windows) or upper-left (Macintosh) corner to close the floating pane.

The Status Bar

Nestled along the bottom of the Document pane, the status bar (**Figure 1.38**) provides yet another set of controls for making your way through a PDF file. The position of these controls makes them easy to access when you're reading straight through a PDF document: You get at them without having to reach across the page. You'll learn more about them later in the chapter.

Full screen view

Hide toolbars

First page

Previous page

Current page

Previous view

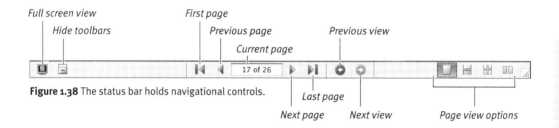

Figure 1.38 The status bar holds navigational controls.

Last page

Next page

Next view

Page view options

Opening and Closing PDF Files

Opening and closing PDF files is straightforward. You can open files whether Acrobat is running or not. As in most applications, there are a number of ways to open and close documents. This section covers my preferred methods.

To open a PDF file from within Acrobat:

◆ Choose Open from the File menu (Ctrl+O/Command+O) to display the Open dialog box; then select the PDF you want to open and click the Open button (**Figure 1.39**).

The file opens.

To open a PDF file outside Acrobat:

◆ Drag the PDF file you want to open onto the Acrobat icon.

   or

   Double-click the PDF's icon.

   The file opens.

To close a PDF file:

◆ Choose Close from the File menu (Ctrl+W/Command+W).

   or

   Click the close box in the document window.

   The file closes. If you've made changes to the document, a dialog box will ask if you want to save the changes before closing the file.

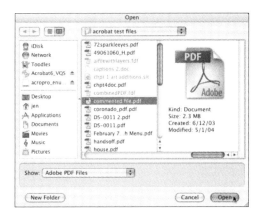

Figure 1.39 Choose the file you want to open and click Open.

Figure 1.40 In Full Screen mode, your document stands alone.

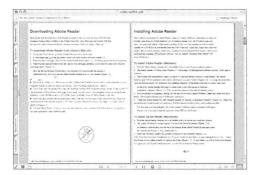

Figure 1.41 Continuous-Facing mode shows two pages across and as many as necessary down.

Viewing a PDF File

Acrobat gives you several options for viewing a PDF. You can view a document without the toolbar and menus, for instance.

To view the document only:

1. Choose Full Screen from the Window menu (Ctrl+L/Command+L).

   Everything but the currently open document will be hidden, including the Acrobat menu bar and any application windows (**Figure 1.40**).

2. To exit Full Screen mode, press the Esc key (or Ctrl+L/Command+L).

   The document will be restored to its previous display, with all the menus, windows, and toolbars.

To view a single page:

◆ Choose View > Page Layout > Single Page.

   or

   Click the Single Page button in the status bar.

   The Document pane will display one page at a time.

To view continuous pages:

◆ Choose View > Page Layout > Continuous.

   or

   Click the Continuous button in the status bar.

   The Document pane will display all the pages in a vertical line as you scroll rather than flip from one page to the next.

To view continuous facing pages:

◆ Choose View > Page Layout > Continuous-Facing.

   The Document pane will display multiple successive pages in two-page spreads across the document window (**Figure 1.41**).

Zooming

Looking at an entire page at once is very convenient for some tasks, but the small text size may make it difficult to read. Fortunately, Acrobat offers a number of zoom options to let you quickly swoop into, and back away from, your document.

There are three basic ways to change the magnification of your document: using tools in the status bar, using the Zoom tools, or using the Dynamic Zoom tool. In the Zoom toolbar, you can choose a preset magnification, use the magnifying glass to click in your document, or select a rectangular area to expand on the Acrobat page. You can also choose a magnification from the status bar and the View menu. Dynamic Zoom lets you use the mouse to zoom in or out.

To magnify a document:

◆ Click the Zoom In tool on the Zoom toolbar (**Figure 1.42**). The magnification increases by a preset amount.

or

Choose Tools > Zoom > Zoom In to select the Zoom In tool. Click in the document to zoom in by a preset amount.

To reduce a document:

◆ Click the Zoom Out tool on the Zoom toolbar to decrease magnification by a preset amount.

or

Choose Tools > Zoom > Zoom Out to select the Zoom Out tool. Click in the document to zoom out by a preset amount.

Figure 1.42 Click the Zoom In tool and you'll be able to enlarge your view of the document.

✔ Tip

■ To zoom out from a specific point, click the Zoom Out tool in the toolbar and click in the Document pane. Or, with the Zoom In tool selected, Alt/Option-click to zoom out by a preset amount or right-click/Control-click for a contextual menu of available magnifications.

ZOOMING

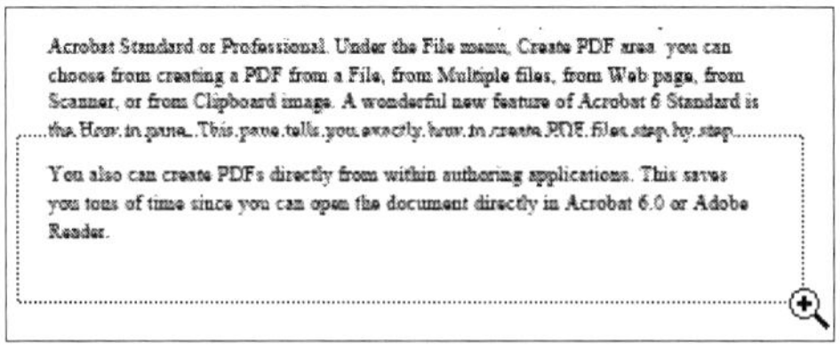

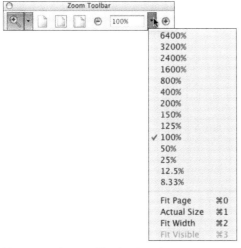

Figure 1.43 Drag a marquee with the Zoom In tool to define an area for enlargement.

Figure 1.44 The magnification drop-down menu presents all your preset choices.

Figure 1.45 Enter your chosen magnification amount in the Zoom To dialog box.

To define the boundaries of the zoomed area:

1. Click the Zoom In tool in the Zoom toolbar.

2. Click and drag your mouse to make a marquee (a dashed-line rectangle) around the area you want to zoom in on (**Figure 1.43**). When you release the mouse button, the selected area will fill the document window.

To zoom to a specific magnification:

◆ Click the downward arrow next to the magnification indicator in the Zoom toolbar (**Figure 1.44**), then select a preset zoom level from the menu that appears.

or

While using either zoom tool, right-click/ Control-click to bring up a contextual menu of the preset magnification choices.

or

Select Zoom To from the View menu (Ctrl+M/Command+M). In the Zoom To dialog box (**Figure 1.45**), enter the magnification percentage you want or select a preset magnification from the pop-up menu, and click OK.

The document will be displayed at the magnification you specified.

✔ Tip

■ You can also zoom to a magnification relative to the document or window size.

◆ Actual Size (Ctrl+1/Command+1) shows the document at 100 percent magnification.

◆ Fit Page (Ctrl+0/Command+0) resizes the document so that its edges just fit in the Document pane.

(continues on next page)

ZOOMING

◆ Fit Width (Ctrl+2/Command+2) resizes the document so that its full width fills the Document pane.

◆ Fit Visible (Ctrl+3/Command+3) resizes the page so that all of its text and graphics fill the Document pane, cutting out blank margin space.

◆ Reflow (Ctrl+4/Command+4) reflows the text in a tagged PDF document one page at a time.

To use the Zoom tools:

1. In the Zoom toolbar, click the tool you wish to use, either Zoom In (the "plus" magnifying glass) or Out (the "minus" magnifying glass) (**Figure 1.46**).

   If the Zoom toolbar isn't visible, choose Tools > Zoom > Zoom Toolbar.

2. Click on the page to zoom in (or out) to the next preset amount.

3. If you want to zoom in on one section of the page, click and drag a marquee around that area on the page with the Zoom In tool.

To use the Dynamic Zoom tool:

1. In the Zoom toolbar, click the Dynamic Zoom tool (**Figure 1.47**).

2. Click on the page and drag up and to the left or right to zoom in. Drag down and to the left or right to zoom out.

To use the Loupe tool:

1. In the Zoom toolbar, click the Loupe tool (**Figure 1.48**).

2. Click to activate the Loupe tool rectangle.

3. Drag the rectangle around to see the zoomed view in the floating pane of the Loupe tool.

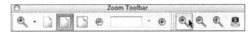

Figure 1.46 Choose the Zoom In tool from the toolbar to magnify your view.

Figure 1.47 The Dynamic Zoom tool is next to Zoom In and Zoom Out on the Zoom toolbar.

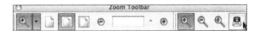

Figure 1.48 The Loupe tool creates its own viewing window.

ZOOMING

Figure 1.49 Tile Horizontally stacks document windows one above another.

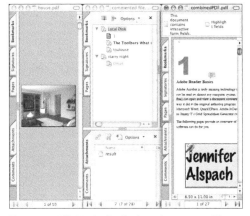

Figure 1.50 Tile Vertically displays documents side by side.

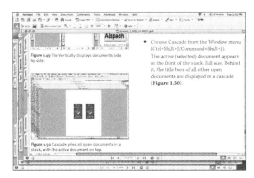

Figure 1.51 Cascade piles all open documents in a stack, with the active document on top.

Arranging Multiple Windows

Your computer screen can get quite messy when you have several PDF document windows open at once. Fortunately, Acrobat offers built-in functions that tidy up your document windows automatically.

To display all open documents:

◆ Choose either Window > Tile > Horizontally (Ctrl+Shift+K/Command+ Shift+K) or Window > Tile > Vertically (Ctrl+Shift+L/Command+Shift+L).

Horizontal tiling displays open documents in a stack of horizontal windows (**Figure 1.49**).

Vertical tiling displays open documents next to each other in vertical windows (**Figure 1.50**).

To bring the active window to the front:

◆ Choose Cascade from the Window menu (Ctrl+Shift+J/Command+Shift+J).

The active (selected) document appears at the front of the stack, full size. Behind it, the title bars of all other open documents are displayed in a cascade (**Figure 1.51**).

Using Split Window view

The split view allows you to see two panes of the same document. It's useful for looking at pages later in the document without losing your place. You can also zoom in or navigate to a different page in one pane without affecting the other pane.

To split the view:

◆ Choose Window > Split.

The window splits into two panes arranged one above the other (**Figure 1.52**). You can now change the page and view displayed in each of these panes without affecting the other pane. To go back to a single pane, choose Window > Split again.

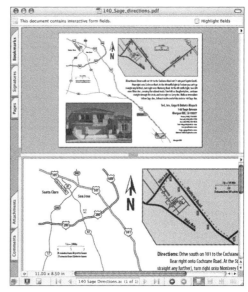

Figure 1.52 Split the window to see two different views of the same document.

ARRANGING MULTIPLE WINDOWS

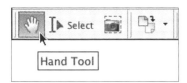

Figure 1.53 Click the hand to grab your document and move it around.

Navigating in a Document Page

You can quickly navigate through any PDF document, using the arrow keys or the buttons provided at the bottom of the document window.

To move up or down within a page:

◆ Press the up or down arrow key.

or

Click and drag the scroll bars along the right side and bottom of the Document pane.

To move a page around:

1. Select the Hand tool from the Basic toolbar (**Figure 1.53**).

The cursor changes to a hand.

2. Click and drag a document page to reposition it.

Release the mouse button, and the page will stay at the new position.

✔ Tip

■ While using any other Acrobat tool, if you want to switch to the Hand tool temporarily, hold down the spacebar. When you're through dragging your page around, release the spacebar to switch back to the tool you were using previously.

Moving Between Document Pages

Moving between pages is as easy as clicking your arrow keys or page buttons. You can also jump directly to a specified page number.

To go to the next page:

◆ Press the Page Down or right arrow key.

  or

  Click the Next Page button in either the Navigation toolbar (**Figure 1.54**) or the status bar.

To go to the previous page:

◆ Press the Page Up or left arrow key.

  or

  Click the Previous Page button in either the Navigation toolbar or the status bar.

To go to a specific page:

1. Choose View > Go To > Page (Ctrl+Shift+N/Command+Shift+N).

   The Go To Page dialog box appears.

2. Enter the number of the page you'd like to go to and click OK (**Figure 1.55**).

✔ Tip

■ You can also type a page number in the Current Page box on the status bar and press Enter/Return to jump to that page.

To go to the first page:

◆ Press Home on your keyboard.

  or

  Click the First Page button in either the Navigation toolbar or the status bar.

To go to the last page:

◆ Press End on your keyboard.

  or

  Click the Last Page button in either the Navigation toolbar or the status bar.

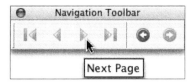

Figure 1.54 You'll find handy navigation buttons in the Navigation toolbar.

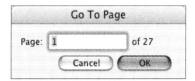

Figure 1.55 The Go To Page dialog box lets you jump instantly to any page.

ACROBAT
IN DEPTH

2

Once you're comfortable with the basics of Acrobat, it's time to move on to some of the more advanced features that make Acrobat such a wonderful tool for working with PDF documents.

Later in the book you'll learn how to create your own PDFs, but first there's a lot more you can do with PDFs that have already been created. For instance, you may want to search a document for a text string and copy text or images. You can even use Acrobat to download and read eBooks. You can also customize Acrobat through the many preference options, such as displaying pages differently and including multimedia in documents.

This chapter takes you on a tour of Acrobat's nitty-gritty details, so you can make this amazing software work for you.

Looking at Document Properties

Each PDF document has certain information associated with it; this data is known by the umbrella term *Document Properties*. It may tell you when the document was created, what application created it, or when it was last modified. Such information comes in handy in a wide variety of ways, from knowing whether you can manipulate a document to knowing what fonts a PDF contains.

Acrobat groups Document Properties into six classes: Description, Security, Fonts, Initial View, Custom, and Advanced.

- The **Description** window contains information about the origin of a PDF file—details like its title and date of creation, the software used to create the original document, and file size and number of pages.

- **Security** shows the security options that were set for the PDF file, such as requiring a password to alter the document, and whether you can print it, copy its content, add comments, fill in form fields, or sign the document.

- **Fonts** lists all of the fonts used in the document.

- **Initial View** shows you how the document will be viewed when you open it. For instance, you can see how the bookmarks panel is displayed, as well as the document's magnification and specific page number. You can also see window and interface viewing options, which let you hide parts of the interface, such as the menu bar and toolbars when a PDF opens.

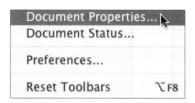

Figure 2.1 Choose Document Properties from the Document pane menu.

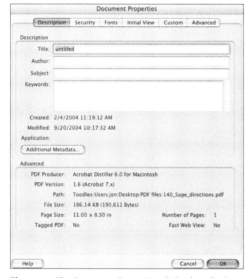

Figure 2.2 The Document Properties dialog box displays information about the currently active document.

◆ **Custom** lets you see if anyone has added custom properties, such as a SerialNumber property, that aren't normally found in the Document Properties.

◆ The **Advanced** options are used by people who create professional documents and include Base URL, Search Index, Trapped, Print Scaling, Binding, and Language.

To read the Document Properties for the current document:

1. Choose File > Document Properties (Ctrl+D/Command+D).

or

Choose Document Properties from the Document pane menu (**Figure 2.1**).

The Document Properties dialog box appears (**Figure 2.2**).

2. Click a topic name to see the details in the window.

3. To close the Document Properties dialog box, click OK or Cancel.

LOOKING AT DOCUMENT PROPERTIES

Checking fonts

The Fonts property lists all of the fonts in the document. You might want to check the fonts in a document to see if they are embedded in the PDF file; if they aren't embedded, Acrobat will substitute a similar font, which may or may not be acceptable in the final document. Note that the font displayed on the screen in a PDF file may be different from the actual font specified in the original design (for instance, Helvetica-Bold is represented on-screen by Arial-BoldMT).

To see the fonts used in a PDF document:

◆ Choose File > Document Properties, and then click the Fonts tab in the Properties dialog box.

A list of all fonts used in the document up to this point appear in the Fonts Used in this Document window (**Figure 2.3**).

Setting other properties

Properties other than Fonts can greatly affect the look, feel, and security of your Acrobat document, so it's important to learn to set them properly. We'll look at these in more detail later in this book.

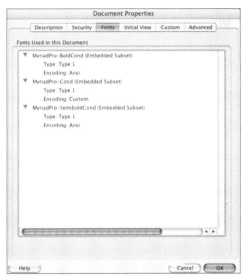

Figure 2.3 You can see a list of all the base fonts used in a PDF document.

Setting Acrobat Preferences

You can change a multitude of preferences in Acrobat that affect the way you view and navigate documents. Although the default preferences work fine for most users, you may want to make some changes. Most of these options can be modified in the Preferences dialog box.

The following list of preferences is not exhaustive, but it does cover the ones you're most likely to use. To take full advantage of Acrobat, be sure to explore the other preferences as well.

◆ **Accessibility** (**Figure 2.4**) lets you change the colors Acrobat uses to display the documents, so that people with vision limitations can read them more easily. To learn about accessibility in detail, see Appendix C.

(continues on next page)

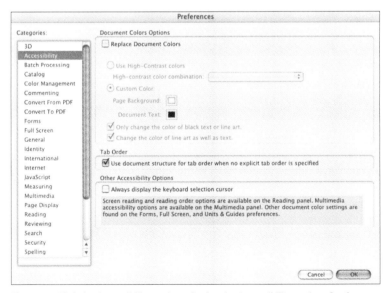

Figure 2.4 Click the Accessibility topic to display the Accessibility options for the currently active document.

- **Batch Processing** lets you specify whether Acrobat should display a confirmation dialog box before executing a pre-recorded set of actions. (Acrobat batch processing lets you record common actions and then repeatedly apply them to one or more Acrobat documents. This would let you, for example, add a watermark to all open Acrobat files or automatically preflight all Acrobat files when they are opened.)

- **Catalog** is where you set indexing options for your PDF documents.

- **Commenting** lets you set the size, opacity, printing, lines, behavior, and locations of comments added to the PDF.

- **Convert From** lets you specify some of the details of how Acrobat converts from PDF to other file types. For example, you can choose the type of compression when exporting a PDF file to a TIFF file.

- **Convert to PDF** lets you specify details of how Acrobat converts from other types of files, such as TIFF files, to a PDF.

- **Forms** settings determine whether forms can automatically calculate values in *fields* (areas of a form in which you can enter information, such as prices and sales tax). The Forms window also contains other options affecting the look of forms.

- **Full Screen** lets you customize Full Screen mode, which is when all Acrobat controls and tools are hidden. The navigation options in the Full Screen window determine how you navigate between pages and quit Full Screen mode. The Full Screen Appearance options let you set the transition styles, background color, and so on.

◆ **General** preferences allow you to set miscellaneous options relating to the user interface, such as how many recently viewed documents you'll see under the File menu, how to label tools and buttons, and how to open other document windows.

◆ **Measuring** allows you to set the snap sensitivity, which is how close you have to be to an object for a tool to snap to it.

◆ **Multimedia** lets you set the preferred media player and certain accessibility options like displaying subtitles and captions with certain types of multimedia.

◆ **Page Display** determines how PDF files are displayed onscreen.

◆ **Reviewing** is the process of sending a file to others to add comments to a PDF. In the Reviewing preferences you can choose the server type, confirm imports, open a comment list, and open toolbars to add your own comments when reviewing a PDF.

◆ **Spelling** lets you opt to have spelling checked while typing and it lets you choose which dictionary to use.

◆ **Startup** is where you set how documents are opened and how the Acrobat application opens.

◆ **TouchUp** lets you choose the Image Editor and Object Editor for editing images with the TouchUp tools. You can also set the TouchUp Reading Order preference.

◆ **Units & Guides** lets you choose whether page measurements are shown in inches, picas, points, centimeters, or millimeters. You can also set the guides location on the PDF and the colors of the guides.

◆ **Web Capture** options help out when you convert a Web page to a PDF, complete with working links. You can set the preferences for opening the file and the options for downloading a secure Web page.

SETTING ACROBAT PREFERENCES

To change Acrobat preferences:

1. Choose Edit > Preferences (Windows) or Acrobat > Preferences (Macintosh), or press Ctrl+K/Command+K.

2. In the left-hand list in the Preferences dialog box, click the Preferences topic you want to set (**Figure 2.5**).

3. Select options and settings in the topic window on the right.

4. Click OK to save your changes or Cancel to close without saving.

✔ Tip

- Keep in mind that changes you make to Acrobat's preferences affect the way you'll view and work with all future documents (unless the document's properties dictate otherwise) within Acrobat. These changes aren't tied to specific documents.

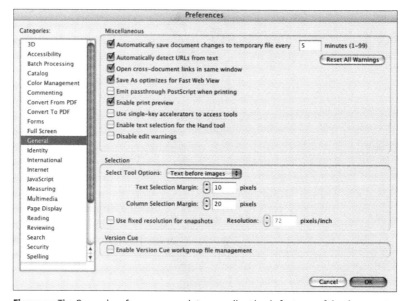

Figure 2.5 The General preferences pane lets you adjust basic features of the document.

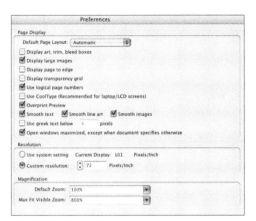

Figure 2.6 Use the Page Display preferences to change the default magnification.

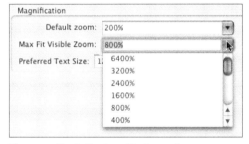

Figure 2.7 Also in the Page Display preferences, you can change the maximum magnification by choosing a preset value or entering your own.

Setting Magnification Preferences

Acrobat displays PDF files at a default magnification that may not be the best for your monitor. Fortunately, you can change this setting within Acrobat's preferences.

To change the default magnification:

1. Open the Preferences dialog box.

2. Choose Page Display from the list on the left.

3. Select a new default magnification level from the Default zoom pull-down menu in the Magnification area (**Figure 2.6**), or type a new percentage in the text box.

4. Click OK.

   All documents will be opened at the new default magnification (unless the document's Open properties specify otherwise).

The Fit Visible option, in which all the visible items—the graphics and text—of a page fill the width of a document window, is great for focusing on the content within a page rather than all the white space around that content. But if you've ever seen Acrobat zoom in too far when you change pages in Fit Visible mode, you'll appreciate Acrobat's ability to restrict Fit Visible's maximum zoom level.

To change the maximum magnification for the Fit Visible option:

1. Open the Preferences dialog box.

2. Choose Page Display from the list on the left.

3. Select a new magnification percentage from the Max Fit Visible Zoom pull-down menu in the Magnification area (**Figure 2.7**), or type a new value in the text box.

4. Click OK.

SETTING MAGNIFICATION PREFERENCES

Reading Notes

With Acrobat and with some documents in Adobe Reader, a user can add comments to a PDF document. This capability is one of the most important features of Acrobat. You can collaborate on a document by using comments to give feedback, such as requesting changes, making important areas pop out, or marking up areas you want removed. Comments can be simple text notes, but they can also be file attachments, sound files, or even movie clips. Notes are probably the most common annotations. You can find more information on commenting and reviewing in Chapters 7 and 8.

To read notes in Acrobat:

1. Locate the note that you wish to read on a PDF document.

   They look like small speech bubbles (**Figure 2.8**).

   Other types of annotations will display different icons, such as a rubber-stamp picture, a microphone, highlighted text, and so on.

2. Double-click the note (or other icon) with the Hand tool to display all of its text (**Figure 2.9**), as well as when and by whom it was written.

3. To close an expanded note, click the close box located in its upper-right corner.

   The note will collapse back to an icon.

✔ Tip

■ Put your cursor over the note instead of double-clicking. This will also show you the note content without having to open the note.

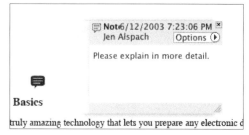

Figure 2.8 A note looks like a little yellow speech bubble.

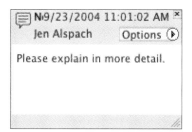

Figure 2.9 Double-click a note to read it.

Figure 2.10 Click the Select tool in the Basic toolbar.

To convert documents to P
Acrobat Standard or Profes
choose from creating a PD
Scanner, or from Clipboard

Figure 2.11 Drag the Select tool across the text you want to select.

Protect Sensitive Business Documents	Adobe Acrobat 6.0 Standard	Adobe Acrobat 6.0 Professional
Secure files with password protection	●	●
Apply permissions with 128-bit encryption	●	●
Approve documents with digital signatures	●	●
Control layer visibility by creating PDF files with layers turned on or off		●
Ensure High-Quality Printed Output		
Divide oversized pages or selected areas of a PDF file into segments for printing	●	●
Preview color separations and transparency flattening		●
Preflight documents to ensure PDF/X compliance and PostScript® level compatibility		●
Embed preflight information directly into a PDF file		●
Print composite output, save composite EPS, or create host-based or in-RIP separations		●
Force all non-white colors to print black when printing documents with light-colored images or lines		●

Figure 2.12 To select only a portion of text, press Ctrl/Command while dragging with the Select tool.

Selecting Text

Suppose you receive a PDF with wonderful content that you'd like to reuse in some other application. Depending on the security options the document's author has set, Acrobat may let you copy text or images, edit an image in the program it was created in, or order prints of the images (once you've gotten permission from the document's creator, of course). However, before you can do anything with text or graphics in a PDF document, you first need to know how to select them. Acrobat offers two tools for selecting text and one for selecting images.

To select text using the Select tool:

1. Choose the Select tool in the Basic toolbar (**Figure 2.10**).

2. Click and drag over the text you want to select (**Figure 2.11**).

    Note that the Select tool lets you select entire words, or just parts of words. After you select the text, a pop-up button appears over the selected text.

3. Place your mouse pointer over the icon and a pop-up menu bar appears giving you options for the selected text (**Figure 2.12**).

    The options are Copy to Clipboard, Replace Text (Comment), Highlight Text, Add Note to Text (Comment), Underline Text, Cross Out Text, Copy As Table, Save As Table, and Open Table in Spreadsheet.

4. Click the option you want.

    The pop-up menu disappears and your text is altered according to the option you chose. If you chose an option that requires a Comment, a comment box appears for you to type your message.

To select text using the Snapshot tool:

1. Choose the Snapshot tool from the Basic toolbar (**Figure 2.13**).

2. Click and drag diagonally across the document, drawing a rectangle around the text you wish to select (**Figure 2.14**).

   This brings up a dialog box telling you the text was copied to the Clipboard (**Figure 2.15**).

✔ Tip

■ The Window menu in Mac OS doesn't contain the Clipboard Viewer command. Instead, go to the Finder and select Edit > Show Clipboard.

To select all text on a page:

◆ Choose Edit > Select All (Ctrl+A/Command+A).

   If the document is displayed in Single-Page mode, all the text of the page on screen is selected. If the document is displayed in Continuous or Continuous-Facing mode, the Select All command selects the entire document.

✔ Tip

■ Remember, you can select and copy text from a document only if its creator has allowed this privilege in the Security options. See Appendix B for more information on security.

Figure 2.13 Click the Snapshot tool to the right of the Select tool.

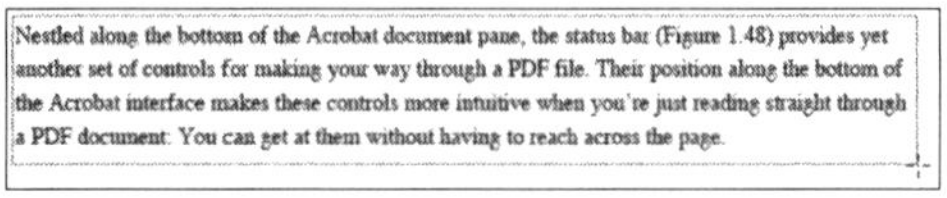

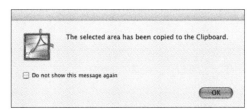

Figure 2.14 Using the Snapshot tool, drag a rectangle around the area of the page you want to select.

![The selected area has been copied to the Clipboard dialog]

Figure 2.15 The dialog box lets you know that the text was copied to the Clipboard.

SELECTING TEXT

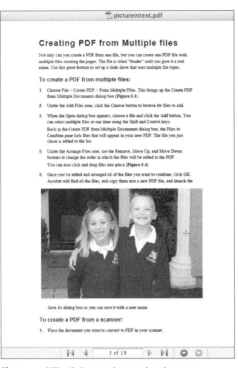

Figure 2.16 The Select tool can select images.

Figure 2.17 Using the Select tool, click on the graphic you want to select. The image appears grayed out.

Selecting Images

The Select tool lets you click on any image and copy it, exactly analogous to the Select tool. If you click on an image, the Select tool selects the entire image, as you would expect. If you click and drag within an image, the tool will select and copy only the area you select.

To select and copy images:

1. Choose the Select tool in the Basic toolbar.

2. With the Select tool, click the image that you would like to select (**Figure 2.16**).

   When you release the mouse button, the selected area is highlighted in gray and a pop-up button appears (**Figure 2.17**).

3. Move your mouse pointer over the pop-up button and a pop-up menu appears with just one choice: Copy to Clipboard.

4. Click on Copy to Clipboard.

   The graphics selection is copied to the Clipboard and available for pasting into another application.

   The text or graphics selection is copied to the Clipboard and available for pasting into another application.

✔ Tip

- To make sure you've actually copied the right material, you can check the contents of the Clipboard. In Windows, choose Window > Show Clipboard; for the Mac OS, go to the Finder and choose Edit > Show Clipboard.

Picture Tasks

A cool set of features in Acrobat is Picture Tasks, which lets you go beyond just selecting and copying images. For example, you can select pictures and pick a layout (choose from a variety of picture packages such as wallet size, 8 x 10, 5 x 7, or a picture package), and then print directly to your printer. The Picture Tasks toolset (**Figure 2.18**) becomes available in the Tasks toolbar when you open a picture created in an Adobe application (JPEG format only). Click the downward arrow next to the Picture Tasks button for a menu of commands (**Figure 2.19**).

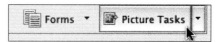

Figure 2.18 The new Picture Tasks tools let you do some pretty cool things.

Figure 2.19 In addition to exporting and printing images, the Picture Tasks let you order prints online.

♦ **Export to Slideshow** lets you create a slideshow from all the pictures in a current PDF file.

♦ **Export Pictures** lets you save images from your PDF file to your computer.

♦ **Export and Edit Pictures** lets you edit images in Photoshop or Photoshop Elements, then save them on your computer.

♦ **Print Pictures** lets you print an image from Acrobat.

♦ **How To Picture Tasks** takes you through each of the above tasks step by step.

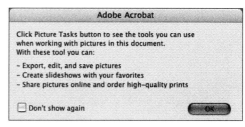

Figure 2.20 Acrobat will describe the Picture Tasks features.

✔ Tip

■ When you open a file that contains an image, Acrobat will display a note telling you about the Picture Tasks features if the images are compatible with Picture Tasks (**Figure 2.20**).

Editing Images

Acrobat enables you to edit images with ease, once you designate a program to use. Acrobat launches that program to open the image to be edited. When it is saved, the updated image shows up in your PDF file.

Images are made up of tiny dots, or pixels. When you edit images, you need to use a pixel-based program (such as Adobe Photoshop or Photoshop Elements) that alters the actual pixels by changing their colors. Objects, or vector-based art, on the other hand, are created by drawing actual lines and creating blocks of colors. You have to use a different type of program—a vector-based program, such as Adobe Illustrator—when you edit these objects or vectors. Use Acrobat to launch a program that lets you edit the images. The image-editing program will save the image temporarily and Acrobat will re-import it into a PDF file. Keep in mind that not all graphics or image-editing applications will work with this feature, such as older versions of GraphicConverter and the current version of Gimp.

To choose image and object editors:

1. Choose Edit > Preferences > General (Ctrl+K/Command+K) to display the General Preferences dialog box.

2. Select the TouchUp option in the list on the left side of the dialog box (**Figure 2.21**).

3. Click the Choose Image Editor button to select your raster-image application (such as Adobe Illustrator) or bitmapped-image application (such as Adobe Photoshop).

4. Locate the program you want to use to edit images and then click Open (**Figure 2.22**).

5. Click the Choose Page/Object Editor button to select your vector-image editing program.

6. Locate the program you want to use to edit images or objects in the PDF document and then click Open (**Figure 2.23**).

7. Click OK in the Preferences dialog box to accept these changes.

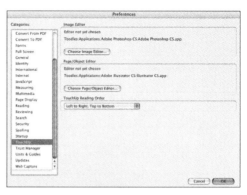

Figure 2.21 Use the TouchUp option to set the applications for fixing images and objects.

Figure 2.22 Once you locate the program, select it and click open to set it as your default application for editing.

Figure 2.23 Locate a different program for your editing of images or objects.

Figure 2.24 You can use the TouchUp Object tool to fix objects.

To edit an object within Acrobat:

1. Using the TouchUp Object tool (**Figure 2.24**), Ctrl+double-click/Option+double-click the object you want to edit.

   The appropriate editor launches for the type of image you want to edit (**Figure 2.25**).

2. Make any changes to your image/object and choose Save from the File menu.

   After you save the file, the changes show up in your PDF file immediately.

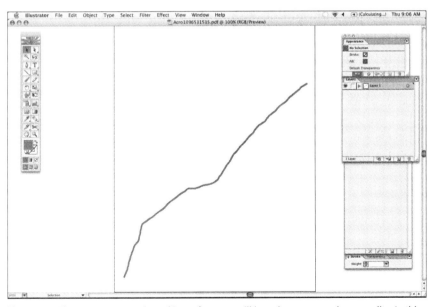

Figure 2.25 The program you selected in preferences will launch so you can do your edits. In this case, the map line needed to be fixed.

Using Digital Editions

Adobe's Digital Editions is a feature in Acrobat that enables you to read eBooks— PDF files saved in a special format—on your computer. It's just like reading and turning the pages of a printed book. With Digital Editions you get the rich text and pictures of a PDF document, but without the complicated interface of Acrobat.

Digital Editions does its best to make you think you're reading a traditional printed book. You can make annotations in your electronic book, add bookmarks at significant passages, and quickly flip to any page. But Digital Editions also includes up-to-date electronic features like searchable text, a built-in dictionary, and a built-in mechanism for downloading additional books. In addition, some eBooks include a license, provided by the seller, that allows you to lend and give your titles to other Digital Editions users, just as you might lend out your favorite paperback novel.

Activating your Digital Editions account

Adobe makes it nearly effortless to activate a Digital Editions account for eBooks. Before you start, make sure you're connected to the Internet so you can access the files you'll need from Adobe's Web site.

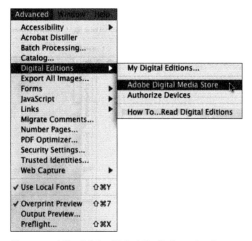

Figure 2.26 The Adobe Digital Media Store is where you can download eBooks.

To activate your Digital account:

1. Choose Advanced > Digital Editions > Adobe Digital Media Store (**Figure 2.26**).

   This takes you to the Welcome to the Digital Media Store Web site.

2. Click on Preview an eBook.

   This will download a free eBook under your Digital Editions. Once the download is complete, you will be asked to activate your account.

3. If you already have an Adobe or .NET Passport account, enter it and the password. If not, you must create an Adobe ID.

4. To create an Adobe ID, follow the easy instructions to complete your activation.

   Once you are signed in, you'll be at the Adobe Store Web site.

USING DIGITAL EDITIONS

Downloading eBooks

At the Adobe Digital Media Store, you can peruse a variety of eBook subjects. Browse, preview, or buy eBooks from various retailers, or try out a book for three days from the Adobe Digital Edition demonstration library. If you're looking for a specific book, take advantage of the Quick Search feature on the Adobe Digital Media Store site, or browse by the genres literature and fiction, mystery and thrillers, and science fiction.

To search Adobe's Digital Media Store:

1. In Acrobat, choose Advanced > Digital Edition > Adobe Digital Media Store.

   This opens the Adobe Digital Media Store Web site (**Figure 2.27**) (http://digitalmediastore.adobe.com).

2. Enter the title of the book or author's name in the Quick Search field, then click the Search button (**Figure 2.28**).

3. The results page shows all eBooks matching your search criteria (**Figure 2.29**).

Figure 2.27 The Digital Media Store is where you'll find many varieties of eBooks.

Figure 2.28 To search for a specific eBook, enter the name of the book or author.

Figure 2.29 The results that matched your search are listed.

Figure 2.30 Click the Preview an eBook link to check out some eBooks.

Figure 2.31 Choose Fiction or Nonfiction.

Figure 2.32 The available titles are listed.

Figure 2.33 Get a brief synopsis of the book.

To download a free eBook:

1. In Acrobat, choose Advanced > Digital Edition > Adobe Digital Media Store. This opens the Adobe Digital Media Store Web site.

2. Click the Preview an eBook link (**Figure 2.30**).

3. Click the Fiction or Nonfiction link to browse the free (preview) eBooks (**Figure 2.31**).

   I chose the Fiction button, and the eBooks available for download were listed in the window (**Figure 2.32**).

4. Click a book title to see information about the book, including its price (free in this case!) and a brief synopsis (**Figure 2.33**).

5. Click the Add to Order button to go to the download page.

6. On the download page, click the Click Here to Download Your eBook link and the book will automatically download into the My Digital Editions window in Acrobat.

   You'll see a progress window as it downloads, and once it's done, a message letting you know that you can now read your eBook.

DOWNLOADING EBOOKS

Purchasing and Organizing eBooks

Currently, a few online booksellers, including eBooks.com, Amazon.com, and Adobe itself, are offering a selection of free titles for trial use with Acrobat, with more available for purchase. Once you've downloaded a few titles, you can organize them into categories.

To purchase an eBook:

1. Choose Advanced > Digital Editions > My Digital Editions.

   The My Digital Editions window appears.

2. Click the Adobe Digital Media Store button (**Figure 2.34**).

3. When the Adobe Digital Media Store Web page opens, choose a genre.

4. Select your book by clicking on the title or the picture of the book's cover.

5. To purchase the book, click the Buy button.

6. If you have finished selecting books, click the Checkout button to complete the purchase.

7. Enter your payment information, then click the Proceed to Downloads button.

   Once your order is processed, you can download the Digital Edition directly into Acrobat.

✔ Tips

- Different vendors have different purchasing methods, so be sure to read and follow the purchasing instructions carefully.

- It's usually a good idea to register with the eBook vendor, even if it's not an actual requirement, so that you don't have to retype your personal information each time you return to the site.

Figure 2.34 Choose the Adobe Digital Media Store button to access eBooks you can purchase.

Figure 2.35 Organize your eBooks.

Organizing your library

Over time, you may accumulate a lot of eBooks in your bookshelf. You may find yourself scrolling through screen after screen of thumbnails, searching for a particular title. But never fear: Acrobat can help.

The toolbar at the top of the My Digital Editions window provides a pop-up menu (**Figure 2.35**) that lets you view your eBooks by category. The categories are assigned when you download an eBook. You can also add a second category to your books. That way, if you have tons of books under the Fiction category, you can subcategorize them as romance, mystery, horror, and so on.

Reading eBooks

Now that you have downloaded an eBook, you can open it up and read it. Once you have a few books in your bookshelf, you'll be able to choose any book to read at your leisure. Acrobat's simple interface makes it easy to view eBooks.

Figure 2.36 Click the Read button to start reading your eBook.

To read an eBook:

1. Choose Advanced > Digital Edition > My Digital Editions.

   The My Digital Editions window appears.

2. Click to select one of the eBooks you downloaded, then click the Read button (**Figure 2.36**).

   or

   Double-click a book in your bookshelf.

   The book opens to display the cover.

3. To turn the page, click the Next Page button in the status bar or press the down arrow on your keyboard.

4. To jump to a specific page, click in the Page Number field in the status bar and type in the page number (**Figure 2.37**).

   or

   Open the Pages pane to display thumbnails of all the book's pages, and click the thumbnail of whichever page you'd like to read.

   The page will be displayed in the reading area.

5. When you've finished reading, choose File > Close (Ctrl+W/Command+W) to close it, or choose Advanced > Digital Editions > My Digital Editions to pick another eBook.

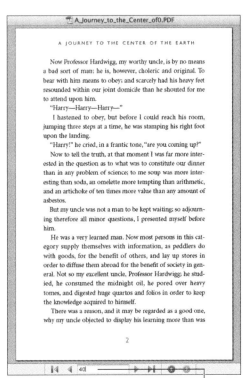

Figure 2.37 Jump to a specific page.

Page Number field

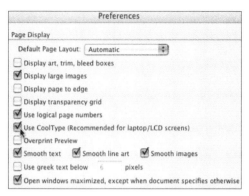

Figure 2.38 Change Preferences to get a better view of your eBook.

Figure 2.39 Rotate the page for a better view.

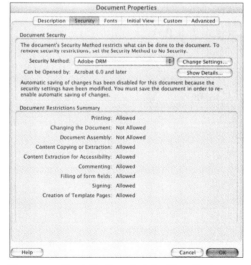

Figure 2.40 Check the Security tab of the eBook.

✔ Tips

■ To enlarge or reduce an eBook's page size, click the Zoom In and Zoom Out buttons in the Zoom toolbar.

■ Acrobat lets you change the look of the text to best suit your screen. In Preferences (Ctrl+K/Command+K) choose the Page Display option on the left. Then check the Use CoolType check box to get better reading text (**Figure 2.38**).

■ You can also have the program read an eBook aloud to you, although the electronic voice may not sound like your ideal narrator. Simply choose View > Read Out Loud > Read This Page Only or Read to End of Document. See Appendix B, "Accessibility," for more information on reading aloud.

■ If you're using a laptop, you may want to rotate your eBook pages 90 degrees for more efficient use of your screen (**Figure 2.39**). Choose View > Rotate View > Counterclockwise. Holding your laptop sideways may not be the most comfortable position, but it's an option.

■ The creators of individual eBooks may restrict users' ability to print or copy text or to lend or give the book to someone else. To check security permissions, choose File > Document Properties, then choose the Security tab (**Figure 2.40**).

READING EBOOKS

Working with Organizer

New to Acrobat 7 is a feature called Organizer, which makes it easy to organize your PDF files. Use Organizer to put a PDF into a collection of PDFs and easily retrieve previously opened files no matter where they are on your hard drive. For instance, Organizer allows you to browse your local disks to find a PDF, and it will help you find a lost file that was created as long as a year ago. Use Organizer to sort PDF files by various criteria such as Name, Title, and Size. You can even use Organizer to start the process of sending a PDF for review. For more on reviewing, see Chapter 9.

You'll find Organizer under the File menu. When you first open Organizer, it can look a bit daunting, but it's easy to use once you understand how it works. There are three panes (**Figure 2.41**). The left pane contains the History area, which lets you see all PDFs you viewed in a certain timeframe.

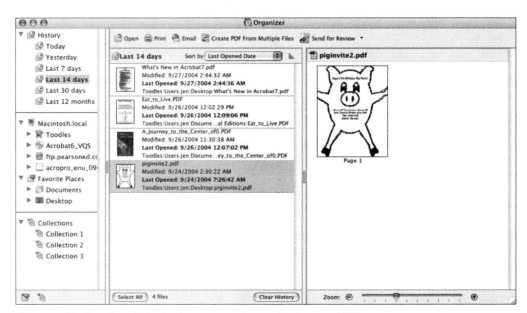

Figure 2.41 The Organizer window is where you can view previously opened PDFs.

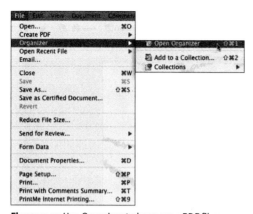

Figure 2.42 Use Organizer to keep your PDF files in Collections.

Underneath the History area is a list of your local disks and Favorite places. Underneath that is a list of *Collections* (groups of PDFs, which you'll learn more about in the next section). The middle pane displays the PDFs from whatever Collection you have selected in the History pane. If you select any of the PDFs from the middle pane, then the pages of those PDFs will show in the third pane.

To open a PDF from Organizer:

1. Choose File > Organizer > Open Organizer (**Figure 2.42**) (Ctrl+Shift+1/ Command+Shift+1).

This brings up the Organizer window.

2. Navigate to the file, then click the Open button.
or
Double-click on the file in the Organizer window.

The file will open in Acrobat (**Figure 2.43**).

✔ Tip

■ Change the way the files are listed by the Sort by pop-up menu found in the middle pane of the Organizer window. Choose to sort by date, file size, or number of pages, among many more options.

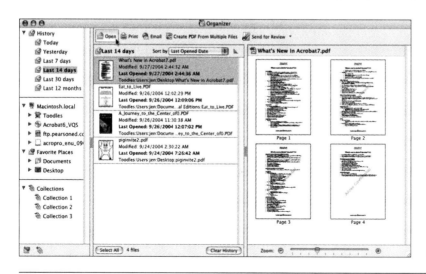

Figure 2.43 Open a previously viewed PDF from the Organizer window.

To send a PDF for review with Organizer:

1. Choose File > Organizer > Open Organizer (Ctrl+Shift+1/Command+Shift+1).

   This launches the Organizer window.

2. Select the file you want to send for review by clicking on it (**Figure 2.44**).

3. Choose the Send by Email for Review option under the Send for Review arrow (**Figure 2.45**).

4. Follow the set of steps in the Send by Email for Review dialog box: click the Next button to go to the next step; enter the email address of the recipient(s) (**Figure 2.46**); click Next and then the Send Invitation button to finish.

   Depending on your email program, Acrobat may generate the email and launch your email browser but not actually send the email message. If that's the case, switch to the email program and click the Send button.

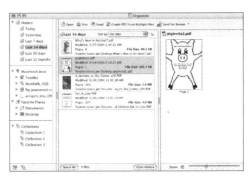

Figure 2.44 Use Organizer to send a PDF for Review. The first step is selecting the file.

Figure 2.45 Opt to use email to send your PDF.

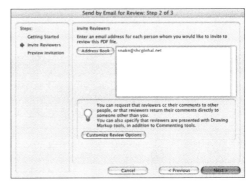

Figure 2.46 Enter the recipient's email address.

Figure 2.47 Rename your collection at any time in the Organizer window.

Figure 2.48 The new name appears in the Collections area.

Working with Collections

A Collection is a group of PDF files that you put together using Organizer. Name your Collections with some common theme, such as work, home, friends, or any theme you wish, and then organize your PDF files into these Collections. Having files with a common theme will make them easy to access (through the Organizer pane), even if they're scattered over different folders on your hard drive. You can rename the default Collections, or create a new Collection. Adding a file to a Collection is as simple as clicking your mouse button.

To rename a Collection:

1. Choose File > Organizer > Open Organizer.

2. Right-click/Control-click or double-click on the collection name.

   The area will be highlighted and ready to rename (**Figure 2.47**).

3. Enter a new name and press Enter or Return.

   The new name will be listed under the Collections (**Figure 2.48**).

To view a Collection:

1. Choose File > Organizer > Open Organizer.

2. Click one time on the Collection name.

   The center pane will list the contents of the selected Collection (**Figure 2.49**).

Figure 2.49 The center pane lists the PDFs in the Collection.

Figure 2.50 Drag the PDF into the Collection folder.

Figure 2.51 The PDF appears in the Collection.

Figure 2.52 Click this button to create a new Collection.

Figure 2.53 The untitled collection is ready to be named.

Figure 2.54 Add as many new Collections as you'd like.

Adding to Collections

Acrobat provides you with three default collection folders. Once you use these up, you can add as many as you'd like. To put it on the Organizer list, simply open the file in Acrobat.

To add a file to a Collection:

1. Choose File > Organizer > Open Organizer.

2. Click and drag the file from the middle pane into the appropriate Collection folder (**Figure 2.50**).

   or

   Drag a file from the Finder (on the Mac) or Windows Explorer (in Windows) into the Collection folder.

   or

   Right-click (Windows) or Control-click (Mac) on a Collection folder, select Add PDF File in the resulting pop-up menu, and navigate to the file you wish to add.

3. Click on the Collection folder to see the file (**Figure 2.51**).

   Add as many files as you want into various Collection folders.

To add a new Collection:

1. Choose File > Organizer > Open Organizer.

2. Click the Create a New Collection button (**Figure 2.52**).

   The new Collection will come up as Untitled and will be highlighted (**Figure 2.53**).

3. Enter a new name and press Enter or Return to see the new Collection (**Figure 2.54**).

ADDING TO COLLECTIONS

SAVING AND PRINTING PDFs

3

Acrobat's ability to let you read a PDF file on almost any computer system is impressive, but you can do even more. You can also edit a PDF's text, add pages, add links, create navigational structures, add comments and edits, send the PDF for reviewing by peers, and even turn a PDF into a multimedia presentation with dazzling transitions between pages. I'll deal with the more complex features in later chapters. For now let's look at how to save PDFs in many formats, reduce file size, make sure a document's ready to print, and finally to print it.

Saving PDF Files in Other Formats

With Acrobat 7, reusing the contents of your PDFs in other programs is easy. You can save a PDF in any of these common formats:

- **PDF (*.PDF)** can be read by everyone with Adobe Reader or Acrobat 7.0.

- **Encapsulated PostScript (EPS)** is best if you plan to use the document as an illustration in a page-layout program. This option saves each page in your PDF as a separate EPS file. You can choose a range of pages.

- **HTML** is best if you plan to put your document on the Web.

- **JPEG, JPEG 2000, PNG,** and **TIFF** are all graphics formats that convert each page of the PDF to a separate bitmapped image file. You lose the ability to edit text when you save a file in these formats. These formats are useful for exchanging high-quality graphics and photographs.

- **Microsoft Word** and **Rich Text Format (RTF)** both allow you to reuse the document's text in a word processor.

- **PNG** stands for Portable Network Graphics. It was created to replace the GIF format but with *lossless compression* (which actually produces larger file sizes). PNG is an image format, so you won't be able to edit a text file if you convert it to this format.

- **PostScript** files contain the printer code that you'd normally send in Acrobat to a high-quality printer. Programmers can use this code to apply a variety of special effects to the printed file.

SAVING PDF FILES IN OTHER FORMATS

Figure 3.1 Choose from a multitude of settings to save your file.

◆ **Plain Text** and **Accessible Text** both convert a document to text only, with no formatting. It's useful for reflowing text into another layout or text application. For example, you can take text from an older PDF document and reflow it into a QuarkXPress, Adobe InDesign, or PageMaker document. Accessible Text preserves comments, form fields, and minor formatting, such as line breaks.

◆ **TIFF** is best to use with pixel-based images and contains a variety of compression methods. When you save your PDF file as a TIFF, you convert it to a series of one-page images.

◆ **XML** is used for high-end forms and document-management systems, for example, when exchanging data among publishing workflows.

To save a PDF in another format:

1. Choose Save As from the File menu (Shift+Ctrl+S/Shift+Command+S).

2. In the Save As dialog box, choose the desired format from the Format pop-up menu (**Figure 3.1**).

3. Click the Settings button to change format-specific parameters for the file (see Acrobat Help for more details).

4. Type a name for the file and choose a location to save it to, then click Save.
   The file is saved in the chosen location with the name you gave it.

SAVING PDF FILES IN OTHER FORMATS

Reducing PDF File Sizes

Sometimes when you're sending files to other users, you need to minimize your file size, making the file as small as possible for transferring. Acrobat can scan through your PDF file, applying a number of strategies to reduce the file's size, while still keeping it readable to a viewer. In some cases, you can reduce the file size by almost 50 percent.

To reduce file size:

1. Open the document for which you want to reduce the file size.

2. Choose File > Reduce File Size (**Figure 3.2**). This brings up the Reduce File Size dialog box (**Figure 3.3**).

3. From the Make compatible with pop-up menu, choose a version of Acrobat you know your recipient can use.

   If you aren't sure what version of Acrobat to choose, you should probably go with Acrobat 4.

4. Click OK.

   This brings up the Save As dialog box so you can give this reduced file a new name and keep the original intact. You can also choose to replace the original file with the smaller file.

Figure 3.2 Reduce your file size by using the Reduce File Size option.

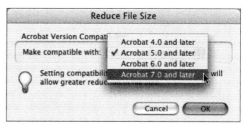

Figure 3.3 Choose the compatible Acrobat application.

Figure 3.4 Use Preflight to check your document before sending it to the service bureau.

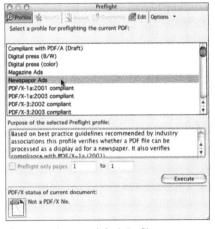

Figure 3.5 Choose a default Profile.

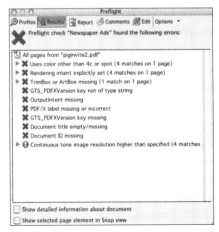

Figure 3.6 The Results area shows the problems in the file.

Preflighting a PDF

Preflight is a wonderful tool in Acrobat that lets you check your file before sending it out to a printer. Preflight checks the PDF document for any issues or problems, such as two different color spaces (RGB and CMYK) or missing fonts, and lets you fix the files before you run into problems at the service bureau. Choose from preset Preflight *profiles* (which dictate the specific criteria that a PDF must conform to) such as Digital Press (B/W), Digital Press (color), Magazine Ads, Newspaper Ads, Acrobat Compatibility, and more. Or you can create your own profile for analyzing the file.

To run Preflight on a PDF:

1. Choose Advanced > Preflight (**Figure 3.4**). This launches the Preflight dialog box.

2. Click on a profile to read about its purpose below the profile box (**Figure 3.5**) and choose the best profile for your document.

3. Click Execute to start the file analysis.

4. Preflight shows the Results of the file listed in the dialog box (**Figure 3.6**).

   With the error information, you can decide what must be changed or left before sending the document out. For example, if you discover RGB images in a file intended for a press, you would need to open those images in an editing program and convert the images to CMYK. Other options you have under Preflight are to create a report from the Preflight file (so that you can pass along the information to someone else), insert Preflight results as Comments (which makes it easier to see the specific elements that are causing trouble on a page), and Edit the Preflight profiles (which you use when you know what you want the preflight mechanism to look for).

Previewing a PDF

Before printing a PDF, whether it's with your own printer or with a professional service bureau, view it onscreen to check for any possible errors or layout issues. You can simulate printing on white paper, view only grayscale (rather than color), and many more options. As you check and uncheck various options, the preview shows in the Document pane so that you can see how the document will look when you print it.

To preview a PDF:

1. Choose Advanced > Output Preview (**Figure 3.7**).

   This launches the Output Preview dialog box. Check the options that you want to view and see the results in the Document pane (**Figure 3.8**). When selecting options, try to match the viewing or printing situation of the document. For example, if it's going to be printed on newsprint, that's what you select.

2. Close the dialog box when you have finished.

Figure 3.7 Preview your PDF before sending it to the printer.

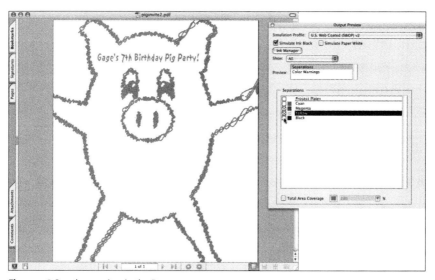

Figure 3.8 See the preview in the Document pane.

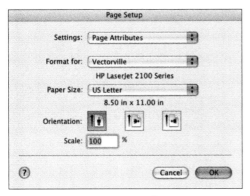

Figure 3.9 Set your page setup information.

Printing PDFs

Printing a PDF to any printer is fairly straightforward.

To set up printing on a Macintosh:

1. Choose Page Setup from the File menu. This opens the Page Setup dialog box.

2. Choose your printer from the pop-up menu.

3. Choose the Paper Size, Orientation, and Scale (**Figure 3.9**).

4. Click OK to accept your selected options and exit the Page Setup dialog box.

To print on a Macintosh:

1. Choose Print from the File menu to open the Print dialog box.

2. Choose your printer from the pop-up menu.

3. Examine the printing options to see if any of them need adjusting. Most of these are standard settings, but some are unique to Acrobat. You should pay special attention to:

   Print What. Should Acrobat print the document, the document and its comments, or only the contents of the fields in a form? Usually you will want to print the document and its comments.

   Page Scaling. Should Acrobat automatically scale your pages to make sure they fit on the page? Usually, you will select None, which yields the fewest surprises.

   Auto-Rotate and Center. Should Acrobat automatically rotate the pages and center them on the paper for the "best" printing results? Leave this unchecked, as it usually results in the printed page being different from what you intended.

4. Click the Print button.

(continues on next page)

To set up and print in Windows:

1. Choose Print from the File menu to open the Print dialog box.

2. From the Name pop-up menu, choose the printer that you want to use.

3. If you want to change any of the printer options, click the Properties button to display the options for your specific printer (**Figure 3.10**).

4. When you've finished changing the printer options, click OK to return to the Print dialog box.

5. Set the print range, number of copies, and any necessary PostScript options, which you will see only if you have a PostScript printer (**Figure 3.11**).

6. Click OK to print the PDF document.

Figure 3.10 Use Properties to change the printer options.

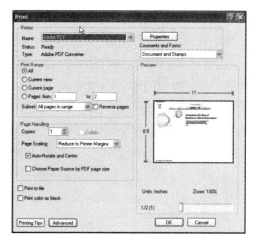

Figure 3.11 Set the range and number of copies.

CREATING PDFs

To convert documents to PDF in Acrobat, you need Acrobat Standard or Professional. You can create a PDF from a single file, multiple files, a Web page, or images from a scanner or the Clipboard. And if you need help, Acrobat's wonderful How To feature can tell you, step by step, exactly how to create PDF files.

You also can create PDFs directly from within authoring applications, such as Photoshop Elements, Microsoft Office, or even Internet Explorer. That means you can save time by creating a PDF without having to open Acrobat or Distiller to convert the file.

Converting a File to PDF

The first step in creating a PDF is to choose your method. From within Acrobat, you can create a PDF from a file, from multiple files, from a scanner, from a Web page, or from a Clipboard image. Pick a creation method from the Create PDF submenu under the File menu (**Figure 4.1**). You can create a PDF from a variety of file types, including BMP, GIF, HTML, JDF, JPEG, JPEG 2000, PICT, PCX, PNG, PostScript/EPS, text file, and TIFF.

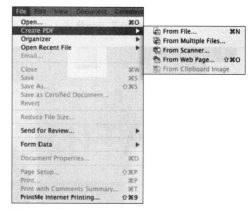

Figure 4.1 The Create PDF submenu has several options.

To create a PDF from a file:

1. In Acrobat, choose File > Create PDF > From File.

   This brings up the Open dialog box.

2. Navigate to the file, then click Open (**Figure 4.2**).

   The file will open in Acrobat.

3. Select File > Save As.

4. Enter a name for the PDF, and select a location where you want to save it.

5. Press Enter/Return or click Save.

   The .pdf extension is automatically added to your filename, and the new PDF is saved at the specified location.

Figure 4.2 Choose the file you want to open as a PDF, then click Open.

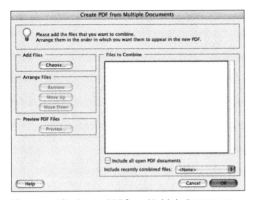

Figure 4.3 The Create PDF from Multiple Documents dialog box looks more complicated than it is.

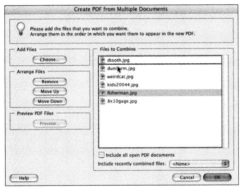

Figure 4.4 You can change the order of documents in your PDF or change your mind about adding a document.

Creating a PDF from Multiple Files

Not only can you create a PDF from a single file, but you can also create a single PDF file from multiple files. Use this great feature to set up a slide show with multiple file types, such as illustrations from Illustrator, photos from Photoshop, and laid-out pages from InDesign.

To create a PDF from multiple files:

1. In Acrobat, choose File > Create PDF > From Multiple Files.

   This brings up the Create PDF from Multiple Documents dialog box (**Figure 4.3**).

2. Under the Add Files area, click the Browse/ Choose button to browse for files to add.

3. When the Open dialog box appears, choose a file and click the Add button.

   You can select multiple files at one time by holding down the Shift key (or Ctrl/ Command if you want to select discontinuous files) while clicking on each file.

   When you click the Add button, you go back to the Create PDF from Multiple Documents dialog box. The file you just chose is added to the list in the Files to Combine pane, which lists the files that will appear in your new PDF.

4. Under the Arrange Files area, use the Remove, Move Up, and Move Down buttons to change the order in which the files will be added to the PDF.

   You can also click and drag files into place (**Figure 4.4**).

   (continues on next page)

CREATING A PDF FROM MULTIPLE FILES

5. Once you've added and arranged all of the files you want to combine, click OK.

Acrobat will find all the files, copy them into a new PDF file, and launch the Save As dialog box so that you can save the file with a new name.

✔ Tip

■ The file is titled "binder" until you give it a real name.

To create a PDF directly from a scanner:

1. Place the document you want to convert to PDF in your scanner.

2. In Acrobat, choose File > Create PDF > From Scanner.

This brings up the Create PDF from Scanner dialog box (**Figure 4.5**).

3. Choose your scanner from the Scanner pop-up menu.

4. Choose Front Sides or Both Sides from the Scan pop-up menu. Set the Destination from the pop-up to either Append to Current Document or New Document.

5. If you are scanning text that you wish to be editable, click the Recognize Text Using OCR box. If you are scanning an image (or text to be saved as an image), leave this box unchecked.

6. Click the Scan button.

The scanned file will open as a new PDF or be added to your open PDF, according to the Destination option you chose.

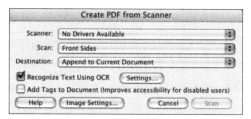

Figure 4.5 In the Create PDF from Scanner dialog box, you can access the settings for compression and compatibility.

Figure 4.6 Enter the URL of the Web site you want to open as a PDF.

Figure 4.7 Acrobat will warn you if the file is very large.

Creating PDFs from Web Pages

You can download a Web page or an entire Web site into Acrobat and convert it into a PDF document. If you first download only a single page or level of the site, and want some of the linked pages later, you can append more pages or levels later.

To create a PDF from a Web page:

1. In Acrobat, choose File > Create PDF > From Web Page (Shift+Ctrl+O/ Shift+Command+O).

   The Create PDF from Web Page dialog box appears.

2. In the URL text field, enter the address of the Web site you want to make into a PDF (**Figure 4.6**).

3. Under the Settings heading, choose how many levels of this site you want Acrobat to download.

   If you select Stay on Same Path or Stay on Same Server, this will keep Acrobat from collecting Web pages from external sites, which can be a problem on pages with links.

   If you select Get Entire Site, you may get a very large PDF document. Acrobat will warn you if that's the case (**Figure 4.7**). Think twice before using this option; getting an entire site will also get all links, and can take many hours.

(continues on next page)

4. Click the Settings button in the Create PDF from Web Page dialog box to open the Web Page Conversion Settings (Windows) or Web Capture Settings (Mac) dialog box. Click the tabs to adjust the General (**Figure 4.8**) and Page Layout (**Figure 4.9**) settings, then click OK.

5. In the Create PDF from Web Page dialog box, click Create to download the Web page and open it as a new PDF file.

✔ Tip

■ You can also access previously saved Web pages on your computer. In the Create PDF from Web Page dialog box, click the Browse button to display any HTML files already saved on your hard drive.

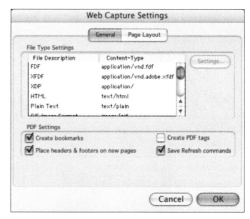

Figure 4.8 Adjust the General settings for your PDF.

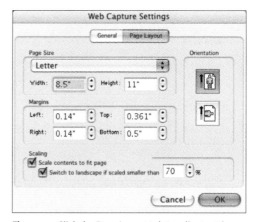

Figure 4.9 Click the Page Layout tab to adjust settings.

Web Page Conversion Settings

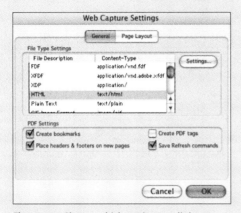

Figure 4.10 Choose which setting to edit in Web Capture.

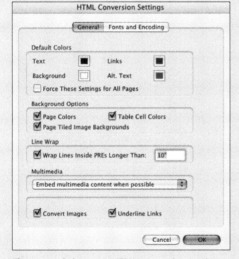

Figure 4.11 Select your HTML conversion setting.

The default settings in Acrobat for converting Web pages to PDFs are probably exactly what you want in most cases. But there may be times when you want to alter them. For instance, you can change the default page size from letter to a custom size, change the scale options, choose a different page orientation, or specify the text and background colors.

The General and Page Layout settings you access through the Create PDF from Web Page dialog box let you choose just how the files download. In the General tab, choose one of the file types and then click the Settings button to alter how Acrobat converts that specific file type.

For example, to change the download settings for an HTML page, click HTML in the File Type Settings list (**Figure 4.10**), then click the Settings button. This opens up the HTML Conversion Settings dialog box (**Figure 4.11**). Here you can set the colors for text and background, and change how Acrobat handles backgrounds, tables, text wrapping, multimedia, links, and images. Once the settings are as you'd like them, click OK to go back to the Web Page Conversion Settings (Windows) or Web Page Capture Settings (Macintosh) dialog box.

Click the Page Layout tab if you want to set the page size, orientation, margins, and scaling. When you're satisfied with all the settings, click OK to go back to the Create PDF from Web Page dialog box.

When you download a Web page as a PDF, it may contain hyperlinks to other Web pages. Clicking the link will open the Specify Weblink Behavior dialog box. Here you choose whether to open the *Weblink* (a link in an Acrobat file to an HTML page on the Web) in Acrobat or in a Web browser.

To open a Web link from within Acrobat:

1. In your active Acrobat document, click a link.

   The Specify Weblink Behavior dialog box appears (**Figure 4.12**).

2. Choose whether you want to open the link in Acrobat or in your Web browser.

3. Click OK and the specified page will open in Acrobat or your browser depending on what setting you chose.

   To change the Weblink Behavior permanently so that linked pages always open in Acrobat or always open in a Web browser, you can adjust your preferences.

4. Choose Edit > Preferences.

   The Preferences dialog box appears.

5. Choose Web Capture from the list on the left.

   The Web Capture settings appear.

6. Choose the desired option from the Open Web Links pop-up menu (**Figure 4.13**) and click OK.

Figure 4.12 Choose the setting for opening Web links.

Figure 4.13 Choose the permanent setting for opening Web links.

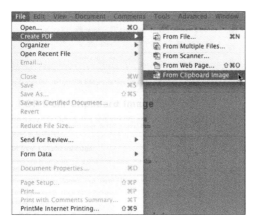

Figure 4.14 You can create a PDF from a Clipboard image.

Figure 4.15 Use the Clipboard image as you would any PDF.

Creating PDFs from Clipboard Images

Any image you copy to the Clipboard can be turned into a PDF using Acrobat. When you create a PDF from a Clipboard image, Acrobat uses the last image you copied to the Clipboard.

To create a PDF from a Clipboard image:

1. Copy the image you want to use in whatever application you choose.

For this example, I copied a selection from Adobe Illustrator.

2. In Acrobat, choose File > Create PDF > From Clipboard Image (**Figure 4.14**).

The Clipboard image is turned into a PDF ready for saving (**Figure 4.15**).

Creating PDFs in Microsoft Office Applications

You can create a PDF directly from a number of Microsoft Office applications using the PDF Maker feature, which is installed on both Windows and Macintosh platforms when you install Acrobat 7.0 Professional.

The steps are essentially the same in all Office applications. The same steps that you follow in Microsoft Word also work for Microsoft Excel, for instance.

To create a PDF from Microsoft Word:

1. Open or create a document in Microsoft Word.

2. Go to View > Toolbars > Adobe Acrobat PDFMaker.

    This makes the PDF Maker 7.0 toolbar appear.

3. Click the Convert to Adobe PDF button in the toolbar (**Figure 4.16**).

    The Save Adobe PDF File As dialog box opens (**Figure 4.17**).

4. Enter a name for the PDF file, choose a save location, and then click the Save button.

    PDFMaker's progress bar will appear to show you when the PDF is complete.

Figure 4.16 Use the Convert to PDF button in the toolbar in Microsoft Word.

Figure 4.17 Save the file as a PDF from Microsoft Word.

Figure 4.18 You can convert a file to PDF using the Print dialog box and choosing the Save as PDF option.

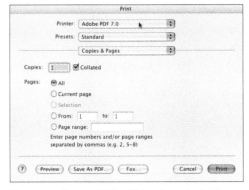

Figure 4.19 Choose Adobe PDF 7.0 from the Printer pop-up menu.

There's more than one way to save a PDF in Microsoft Office applications. The following method works in Office, but also in many other applications.

To create a PDF with the Adobe PDF printer:

1. In any of the Microsoft Office applications (Word, Excel, or PowerPoint), open the file you want to convert.

I use Microsoft Word for this example.

2. Choose File > Print to open the Print dialog box (**Figure 4.18**).

3. Choose Adobe PDF 7.0 from the Printer pop-up menu at the top of the dialog box (**Figure 4.19**).

4. Click the Save As PDF button to bring up the Save to File dialog box.

5. Enter a name for the file, choose a destination, then click Save to save the file as a PDF.

6. The file does not automatically open in Acrobat.

If you want to open the file you have just created, choose File > Open in Acrobat or double-click on the document you saved.

PDFs in Office Applications

Creating PDFs in Other Applications

You can generate a PDF directly from within many other authoring applications. You no longer have to first save the file as a PostScript file, as you did in previous versions of Acrobat. Acrobat now provides several ways to do this as simply as possible.

On the Windows platform, you can create a PDF directly from the following programs: Autodesk AutoCAD, Microsoft Access, Excel, Internet Explorer, Outlook Express, PowerPoint, Publisher, Project, Visio, and Word. The steps to create a PDF in each of these applications are pretty much the same. Each program has a Create PDF button. When you click that button and save the file, you have a PDF.

You can create one-button PDFs on the Mac in only the Microsoft Office products, but there are many other applications, such as Adobe Photoshop and Illustrator, that give you other methods for creating PDFs.

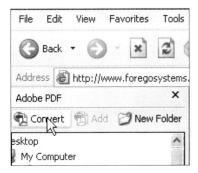

Figure 4.20 You can also convert a Web page from Internet Explorer.

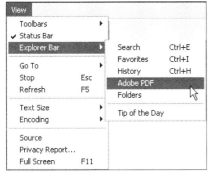

Figure 4.21 You may have to open the toolbar from the menu.

To create a PDF from within Internet Explorer (Windows):

1. In Internet Explorer, go to the Web page you want to convert to a PDF.

2. Click the Convert button (**Figure 4.20**) to open the Convert Web Page to Adobe PDF dialog box.

   If you have Windows XP and don't see the PDF icon, choose View > Explorer Bar > Adobe PDF (**Figure 4.21**).

3. In the Convert Web Page to Adobe PDF dialog box, enter a filename, choose a location, and click Save.

   Once you click the Save button, Internet Explorer will save the Web page as a PDF in the location you chose, and you can open it with Acrobat.

To create a PDF from within Photoshop or Illustrator:

1. In Photoshop or Illustrator, choose File > Save As.

   This launches the Save As dialog box.

2. Enter a name for the file and in the format pop-up, choose Photoshop PDF or Adobe PDF.

3. Click the Save button and you have just created a PDF.

CREATING PDFs IN OTHER APPLICATIONS

Using Distiller

In some programs, and for greater control over the quality of your PDF, you will still need to create PDFs the old-fashioned way: by creating a PostScript (PS) or Encapsulated PostScript (EPS) file first and converting it with Acrobat Distiller. (Graphics professionals are usually the only ones who need to use Distiller.)

Distiller is a PostScript-to-PDF converter that is used behind the scenes by the Adobe PDF printer to make PDF files. You can also use it as a stand-alone application to make PDF files from your own PostScript and EPS files. You would do this when you need sophisticated control over the characteristics of your PDF file, such as the way fonts are embedded, or how images are compressed.

To distill a PostScript file into a PDF file:

1. In Acrobat, choose Advanced > Acrobat Distiller (**Figure 4.22**).

2. From the Default Settings menu, choose from the presets depending on how your PDF will be viewed (**Figure 4.23**).

   ▲ High Quality Print will create a higher resolution for the PDF than the standard. Grayscale and color images will print at 300 dpi and monochromatic images at 1200 dpi.

   ▲ PDF/A will enable the PDF to contain only text, images, and vectors. It doesn't allow encryption, and embedded text must be in accordance with the PDF/A compliance.

   ▲ Press Quality creates a file ready for press printing with grayscale and color images at 300 dpi and monochrome images at 1200 dpi.

Figure 4.22 You can still make a PostScript file into a PDF via Distiller.

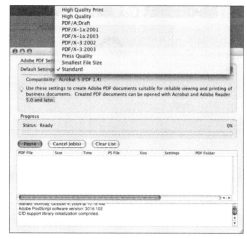

Figure 4.23 Under the default settings, you can select a preset.

Figure 4.24 Navigate to the file you want and open it in Distiller.

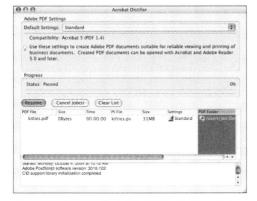

Figure 4.25 See your file in listed in the Distiller window.

Figure 4.26 Watch the progress of your file.

▲ **Smallest File Size** creates a file specifically for viewing on the Web. It makes the file size as small as possible by using compression, downsampling, and low-image resolution.

▲ **Standard** creates a PDF that is to be printed on copiers or desktop printers or sent as a proof. It doesn't create a high-quality print, like those from commercial printers, but a good desktop-printer quality print.

3. In Distiller, choose File > Open.

4. Navigate to the PostScript file you want to distill and then click the Open button (**Figure 4.24**).

The file appears in the list in the Acrobat Distiller dialog box (**Figure 4.25**).

5. Select the file you want to distill from the list and click the Resume button.

The Acrobat Distiller window shows the progress of the distillation (**Figure 4.26**). You'll notice that Distiller has created a new file in the same place where you have stored the initial file.

When the process is finished, you can close the window or choose Quit from the File menu (Ctrl+Q/Command+Q) to exit Distiller. Use Acrobat to open the file.

✔ Tip

■ As a PostScript file is being distilled, notes that you might find useful show up at the bottom of the Acrobat Distiller window below the Progress bar. These notes include the name of the file, when the distilling process started, the location of the original PostScript file, the destination folder or directory of the new PDF file, and font substitutions (if any).

USING DISTILLER

To change Distiller preferences:

1. In Distiller, choose Distiller > Preferences (Ctrl+K/Command+K) (**Figure 4.27**).

   The Preferences dialog box appears (**Figure 4.28**).

2. To turn each option on or off, click the appropriate check box.

   Here are the options you can set:

   ▲ **Notify When Watched Folders Are Unavailable** will make a dialog box appear if a "watched" folder is not available. Unless Distiller is being run on a server, keeping this option checked is a good idea. (Watched folders are discussed later in this chapter.)

   ▲ **Notify when Windows TEMP Folder Is Nearly Full** tells Distiller to prompt you when the TEMP folder is almost full so you can rearrange files to make more room, by moving files out of this folder (Windows only).

   ▲ **Ask for PDF File Destination** tells Distiller to prompt you for the location to save the PDF file.

   ▲ **Ask to Replace Existing PDF File** makes Distiller ask you for permission before overwriting a file with the same name.

   ▲ **View PDF When Using Distiller** causes the newly created PDF to be displayed as soon as Distiller finishes its job.

   ▲ **Delete Log Files for Successful Jobs** means that Distiller will remove the log file for jobs that were distilled with no errors.

Figure 4.27 Under the Distiller menu you can set Preferences for Distiller.

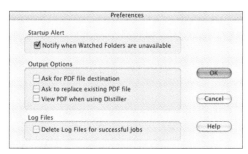

Figure 4.28 Use the Preferences dialog box to set how you want Distiller to perform.

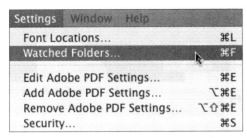

Figure 4.29 You can automatically create PDFs from PostScript files by making a watched folder.

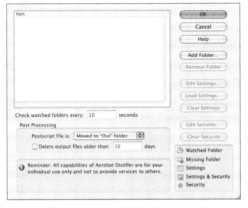

Figure 4.30 Enter your settings in the Watched Folders dialog box.

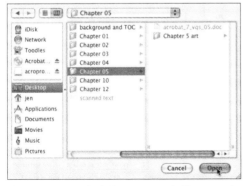

Figure 4.31 Select the folder you want Distiller to watch.

Automating Distiller

You can set up Acrobat Distiller to distill PostScript files into PDF files automatically.

Two steps are involved in automating Distiller. First, the Distiller application itself must be running. Second, the PostScript files need to be placed in a "watched" folder from which Distiller can convert the files.

Distiller can be set up to find PostScript files in specified folders. If you have a folder set up as a watched folder, the program automatically converts any PostScript file dropped into that folder to a PDF document.

To make a watched folder:

1. In Distiller, choose Watched Folders from the Settings menu (Ctrl+F/Command-F) (**Figure 4.29**).

   The Watched Folders dialog box appears (**Figure 4.30**).

2. Click Add Folder to display the Open dialog box.

3. Select the folder that you want Distiller to watch and then click Open (**Figure 4.31**).

4. Click OK in the Watched Folders dialog box.

From this point forward, whenever Distiller is running, any PostScript files that you placed in the designated watched folder will be converted to PDF documents automatically.

STRUCTURING PDF DOCUMENTS

PDF documents are ready to go immediately after you create them, but you can do all sorts of things to make the files more readable and easier to use. Adobe Acrobat provides several options for customizing PDF documents.

This chapter covers some of the changes you can make in PDF files to individual pages or to the entire document—everything from controlling what page shows when you open the document to changing the order of pages or combining two PDFs into one. When you've finished working with Acrobat, remember to save your documents so that they include your latest changes.

Changing Open Options

By default, Acrobat opens PDF files to the first page and at the Fit in Window magnification level. At times, however, you want a document to open to a different page or at a different magnification level. Setting these properties in Document Properties affects only the current document; the same properties can also be set among the Acrobat preferences, in which case they apply to all documents (unless overridden by the document).

In the Initial View pane of Document Properties, you can change settings not only for your pages, but also for the window it opens in and the entire user interface. These controls allow you to display or hide most parts of the user interface (the toolbars, the menu bar, etc.). But you can't rearrange controls or pick and choose particular toolbar buttons. Here are a few examples:

◆ The Document Options' **Show** pull-down menu provides a choice of showing the Page only, the Bookmarks pane and Page, the Pages pane and page, Attachments Pane and Page, or Layers pane and Page.

◆ From the **Show** pull-down menu in the Window Options area, choose what Acrobat will display in the title bar; your choices are the title of the PDF document (as listed in the document summary) or the document's filename.

◆ **Hide Window Controls** removes the scroll bars and the close and resize boxes from view. You can get these controls back only by unchecking this option, saving the document, and then closing and reopening the document.

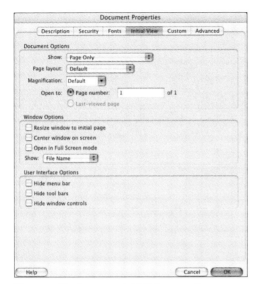

Figure 5.1 The Document Initial View pane lets you choose how your documents open.

To change the way a file opens:

1. Choose File > Document Properties. Click the Initial View tab.

   The Initial View pane of Document Properties is displayed (**Figure 5.1**).

2. Make your changes.

   You can specify which page the document will open to and what interface elements will be visible.

3. Click OK.

4. Save the document by choosing File > Save (Ctrl+S/Command+S).

   The next time someone opens the document in Acrobat, it will look the way you specified.

✔ Tip

■ To set a new magnification level, type a specific value in the Magnification text field or make a selection from the pull-down menu (click the triangle next to the field).

Working with Thumbnails

Thumbnails provide a quick visual method of going to another page. If you are on page 1 and want to get to page 12 quickly, you can just click the thumbnail for page 12. Each thumbnail is a tiny representation of a page. Clicking a thumbnail instantly takes you to that page at the current magnification level.

Thumbnails are not stored in a PDF by default, because they add to the document's file size, but they are generated on the fly when you open the Pages pane. These thumbnails will not be saved when the document is closed, however. If you want to make sure that thumbnails are always present in the document, you can embed them.

To view and use thumbnails:

1. Choose View > Navigation Tabs > Pages (**Figure 5.2**).

   The Pages pane on the left side of the document opens and, after a short delay, displays thumbnails of the pages in the vicinity of the current page (**Figure 5.3**).

2. Click the thumbnail for the page you want. You move to that page instantly.

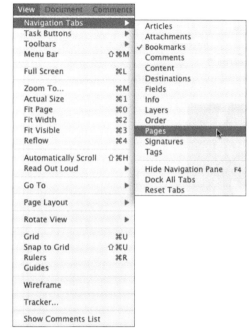

Figure 5.2 Choose View > Navigation Tabs > Pages to display the Pages pane.

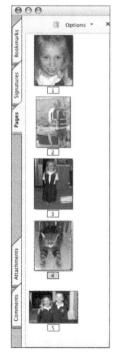

Figure 5.3 The Pages pane is displayed on the left side of the application.

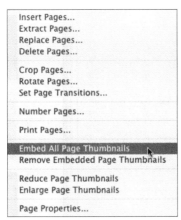

Figure 5.4 Choose Embed All Page Thumbnails from the Pages pane Options pop-up menu.

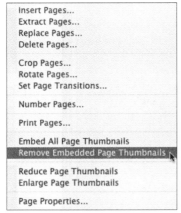

Figure 5.5 To delete thumbnails, choose Remove Embedded Page Thumbnails from the Pages pane Options pop-up menu.

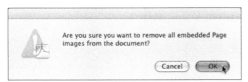

Figure 5.6 This dialog box asks for confirmation before deleting thumbnails.

To embed thumbnails in a document:

1. Choose View > Navigation Tabs > Pages.
   or
   Click the Pages tab along the left edge of the document.

2. Choose Embed All Page Thumbnails from the Pages pane pop-up menu (**Figure 5.4**).

   Acrobat creates thumbnails for every page in the document and stores them permanently within the PDF. Now thumbnails will be displayed immediately when you move to a different part of the document, rather than after a delay.

To delete thumbnails:

1. Choose Remove Embedded Page Thumbnails from the Pages pane pop-up menu (Figure 5.5).

   A dialog box appears, asking whether you're sure that you want to remove the thumbnails.

2. Click OK (**Figure 5.6**).

✔ Tip

■ After you edit a PDF document with embedded page thumbnails, you must remove them and then embed a fresh set, so they reflect the changes you made in the document.

Changing Page Order and Numbers

Shuffling pages around within a PDF document is as simple as dragging and dropping, thanks to the magical goodness of thumbnails.

To reorder pages within a PDF:

1. With the document open and page thumbnails showing, click to select the thumbnail of the page or pages you want to reorder (**Figure 5.7**).

2. Drag to the point where you want to move the page.

   A blue bar marks the spot.

3. Release the mouse button to drop the pages in their new location.

   The pages are renumbered to accommodate the move (**Figure 5.8**).

✔ Tips

- Hold down Ctrl+Alt/Command+Option while dragging to move a copy of the selected pages to the new location, while the original pages remain in place.

- You may select and move a group of non-consecutive pages, but they will be consecutive after you drop the pages in their new location.

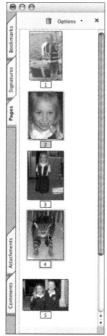

Figure 5.7 Select the thumbnails of the pages you'd like to move.

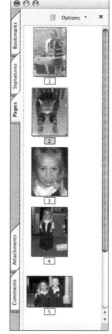

Figure 5.8 The moved pages are now in their new location.

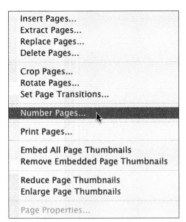

Figure 5.9 The Number Pages command is in the Pages pane Options pop-up menu.

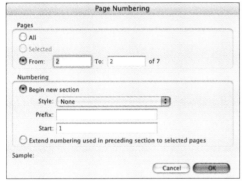

Figure 5.10 The Page Numbering dialog box offers many choices for custom numbering schemes.

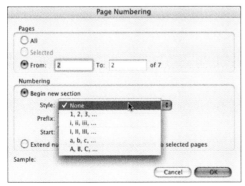

Figure 5.11 Choose a numbering style.

Occasionally, you may want to impose a custom page-numbering scheme on a document.

To renumber pages:

1. Choose Number Pages from the Pages pane Options menu (**Figure 5.9**).

   The Page Numbering dialog box opens (**Figure 5.10**).

2. Choose which pages you want to renumber: All, Selected, or a range of pages.

3. If you want to continue the same numbering that was used in the preceding section, click the Extend Numbering Used radio button. Acrobat will refer to the numbering of the previous section and continue from that.

   or

   If you want to use a new sequence of numbers in these pages, click Begin New Section; then choose a numbering style from the pop-up menu (**Figure 5.11**), a prefix for the page numbers (if desired), and a number to start the sequence. Use this option if you are trying to keep an accurate account of each section's page counts. For example, if you are separating the sections into chapters and you want each chapter to have its own numbering, use this feature.

✔ Tips

- If you prefer to see the default numbering system in Pages pane and status bar rather than your custom numbering system, uncheck Use Logical Page Numbers in the Page Display area of the Preferences dialog box (Ctrl+K/Command+K).

- These page numbers will appear in the Window controls at the bottom of the document window, not as numbers on the document's pages.

Inserting and Replacing PDF Pages

Often, you may want to move pages from one document to another or combine multiple PDFs into a single document. Acrobat provides two ways to accomplish these tasks. One method involves menu commands; the other requires you to simply drag and drop page thumbnails.

To insert one PDF document into another:

1. While you have a document open, choose Document > Insert Pages (Ctrl+Shift+I/Command+Shift+I).

   or

   Choose Insert Pages from the Pages palette Options menu (**Figure 5.12**).

   The Select File to Insert dialog box appears (**Figure 5.13**).

2. Navigate to the file you'd like to insert into the current document, then click Select.

   The Insert Pages dialog box appears (**Figure 5.14**).

3. In the Page portion of the dialog box, specify where you want the pages to be inserted. Click the First or Last radio button, or type a number in the Page text field.

4. From the Location menu, choose whether the document will be inserted before or after the page you chose.

5. Click OK.

   The pages will be inserted at the document location you selected.

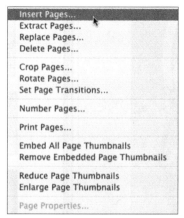

Figure 5.12 To insert pages into a file, choose Insert Pages from the Pages pane Options menu.

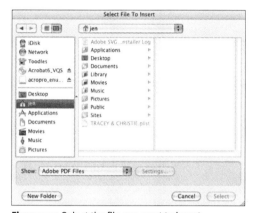

Figure 5.13 Select the file you want to insert.

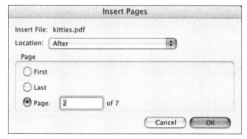

Figure 5.14 Specify where you want to insert the file.

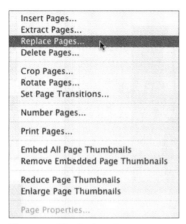

Figure 5.15 The Replace Pages command is in the Options menu.

Figure 5.16 Select the file that contains the replacement pages.

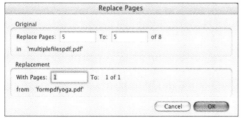

Figure 5.17 Indicate which pages you want replaced, as well as the pages that will replace them.

✔ Tip

■ If you don't want to insert the entire contents of a file, you'll have to open that file and extract the pages you want to insert in a new file. (Extracting pages is explained later in this chapter.) Be sure to use a distinctive name for the file that contains the extracted pages, so you don't confuse it with the whole document.

To replace one PDF page with another:

1. Start with a document in which you want to place new pages.

2. Choose Document > Replace Pages.

   or

   Choose Replace Pages from the Pages palette Options menu (**Figure 5.15**). The Select File with New Pages dialog box appears.

3. Select the file that contains the replacement pages; then click Select (**Figure 5.16**). The Replace Pages dialog box appears.

4. In the text fields in the Original section (**Figure 5.17**), type the page numbers of the range of pages you want to replace in the open document.

   This range determines the number of pages that will be taken from the replacement document. You can replace only the same number of pages.

5. In the Replacement text field, type the number of the first replacement page.

   Acrobat automatically calculates the range of pages needed to replace the pages you have chosen in the original file.

(continues on next page)

INSERTING AND REPLACING PDF PAGES

6. Click OK.

A warning will appear asking if you really want to replace those pages.

7. Click Yes.

The specified pages of the open document are replaced.

✔ Tip

- You'll have to replace noncontiguous pages separately. To insert pages 1 and 5 from a replacement document, for example, you'll need to perform the Replace Pages process twice.

Moving pages as thumbnails

You'll usually find that page thumbnails provide an easier way to move individual pages between PDFs.

To copy pages from one document to another:

1. Open both the document into which you want to copy pages (the original document) and the document from which you want to copy pages (the source document).

2. Open the Navigation pane of each window and arrange them so that both documents are visible, with the source document active (**Figure 5.18**).

3. In the source document, select the thumbnails of the pages you want to copy. (Shift-click to select consecutive pages; Ctrl-click/Command-click to select nonconsecutive pages.)

A faint blue outline appears around the selected pages (**Figure 5.19**).

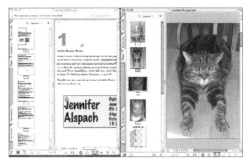

Figure 5.18 Line up the two documents side by side with their Navigation panes open.

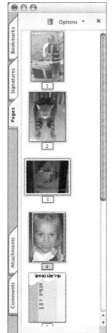

Figure 5.19 Select pages to copy to the other document. In this document, pages 1 through 4 are selected.

Figure 5.20 Drag pages from the source document's Navigation pane to the original's.

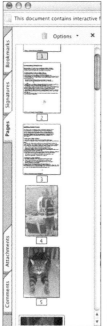

Figure 5.21 The pages are copied, and page numbers are recalculated.

4. Drag the selected page thumbnails into the Pages palette of the original document.

You'll see a light blue line where you are inserting the new page in the other PDF document (**Figure 5.20**).

5. Release the mouse button when the arrow is over the spot where you want to insert the pages.

As the arrow moves over a spot between pages, a blue bar appears. The pages are copied from the source document to the original document, and the pages in the original document are renumbered (**Figure 5.21**).

✔ Tips

- To move pages (rather than copy them) from one document to another, follow the same procedure, but hold down Ctrl+Alt/Command+Option while dragging. This method inserts the page into the original document and removes it from the source document. Afterward, pages in both documents are renumbered.

- This method works only when the Pages pane is docked, not floating.

To replace one PDF page with another:

1. Display the Pages panes of both the source and original documents.

2. In the source document, select the thumbnails of the replacement pages.

3. Drag the selected thumbnails into the Pages pane of the original document, positioning the mouse pointer over the page number of the first page you want to replace.

    The pages that will be replaced turn black (**Figure 5.22**).

4. Release the mouse button.

    The pages from the source document replace an equal number of pages in the original document (**Figure 5.23**).

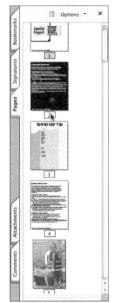

Figure 5.22 Drag the replacement page's thumbnails into the Pages palette of the original document.

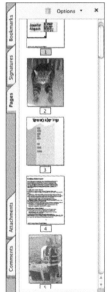

Figure 5.23 The page is replaced.

INSERTING AND REPLACING PDF PAGES

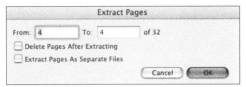

Figure 5.24 Enter the pages to remove in the Extract Pages dialog box.

Removing PDF Pages

You can export selected pages from a PDF document to a new document. You can also use this process—called *extracting* in Acrobat—to remove pages as you export them. In effect, extracting breaks a PDF document into smaller documents.

To extract pages from a PDF document:

1. Choose Document > Extract Pages.

   or

   Choose Extract Pages from the Pages palette Options menu.

   The Extract Pages dialog box appears (**Figure 5.24**).

2. In the text fields, type the page numbers of the page or range of pages you want to extract from the active document.

   Alternatively, select the thumbnails of the pages you want to extract before using the Extract Pages command. The range you selected will be displayed in the dialog box.

3. If you want Acrobat to delete the extracted pages from the document, make sure that the Delete Pages After Extracting check box is checked.

4. Click OK.

   A new document containing the extracted pages opens. This new document is automatically named "Pages from *original document name*." The document has not been saved at this point, so be sure to rename and save it before closing the file or exiting Acrobat.

Although you can use extracting to remove pages from a PDF document, the process also creates a new document that you may not need. Sometimes, you just want to get rid of pages. Acrobat lets you do so with the Delete Pages command.

Figure 5.25 Specify which pages you want to delete.

To delete pages from a PDF document:

1. Choose Document > Delete Pages (Ctrl+Shift+D/Command+Shift+D)

   or

   Choose Delete Pages from the Pages pane Options pop-up menu.

   The Delete Pages dialog box appears (**Figure 5.25**).

2. In the text fields, type the page numbers of the page or range of pages you want to delete.

3. Click OK.

   A dialog box appears, asking whether you're sure that you want to delete the specified pages (**Figure 5.26**).

4. If you are sure, click OK.

   The pages will be deleted.

Figure 5.26 Click OK if you're sure you want to delete the pages.

✔ Tip

- You can delete pages from a PDF document using the page thumbnails. Select the thumbnails of the pages you want to delete and then press Backspace or Delete. When the confirmation dialog box appears, click Yes to delete the pages.

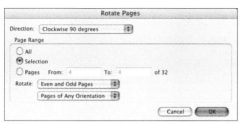

Figure 5.27 In the Rotate Pages dialog box, specify the pages to be rotated and the direction of the rotation.

Rotating and Cropping Pages

Occasionally, a PDF page will be rotated the wrong way when it opens in Acrobat. You can fix that in the Rotate Pages dialog box.

To rotate a PDF page:

1. Choose Document > Rotate (Ctrl+Shift+R/Command+Shift+R).

or

Choose Rotate from the Pages palette Options pop-up menu.

The Rotate Pages dialog box appears.

2. Specify the direction you want to rotate the pages (**Figure 5.27**).

3. Specify the page or range of pages to be rotated.

You can use the pop-up menus at the bottom of the dialog box to narrow your choice of pages, for example, rotating only even pages or only pages currently in landscape orientation.

4. Click OK.

The pages are rotated.

✔ Tip

■ To rotate several sets of noncontiguous pages, you'll have to handle each contiguous set separately.

PDF pages created in a different application (such as Microsoft Word, Adobe Illustrator, or Adobe Photoshop) may contain areas that you don't need. Acrobat provides a convenient way to crop out these areas.

To crop a PDF page:

1. Choose Document > Crop (Ctrl+Shift+T/Command+Shift+T).

   or

   Choose Crop Pages from the Pages pane Options pop-up menu (**Figure 5.28**).

   or

   Click the Crop tool in the Advanced Editing toolbar, drag across the page to define the boundaries of the crop, and press Enter or Return. If the Crop tool is not visible, choose Tools > Advanced Editing > Advanced Editing Toolbar. The Advanced Editing toolbar with the Crop tool will appear as a floating palette (**Figure 5.29**).

   Whichever method you use, the Crop Pages dialog box appears (**Figure 5.30**).

2. In the Crop Margins Margin Control fields, type the amount you want to crop from each page's edge (or select the distances by clicking the up and down arrows by each box).

   As you change these numbers, a black line appears on the document thumbnail at the center of the dialog box, giving you a preview of the new margins. At the same time, a dotted line appears on the document at each of the margins being cropped.

3. If you don't like what you've chosen and want to start over, click the Set to Zero button to remove all changes.

   If you previously defined a cropping area with the Crop tool and then changed it in the dialog box, you can return to the original selection by clicking the Revert to Selection button.

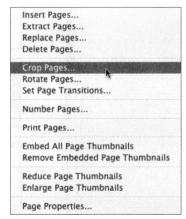

Figure 5.28 To crop pages you can use the command in the Pages palette's Options menu...

Figure 5.29 ...or the Crop tool in the Advanced Editing toolbar.

4. In the Page Range section, select the pages to be cropped.

In addition to cropping every page or only selected pages, you can crop only even or odd pages by selecting that option from the Crop pop-up menu.

5. Click OK.

A dialog box appears, asking whether you really want to crop the selected pages.

6. Click Yes to crop the pages as you've indicated, or click No to leave the document untouched.

✔ Tip

■ You cannot undo a cropping action, but if you choose Revert from the File menu, Acrobat will revert to the last saved version of the PDF document. Keep in mind that if you save and reopen the document later, you have no way to retrieve the areas that you've cropped, even if you use the Revert command.

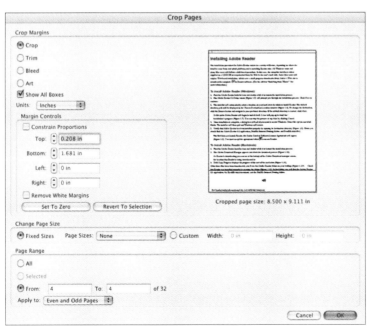

Figure 5.30 In the Crop Pages dialog box, enter numbers for the new margins and specify which pages will be cropped.

Adding Headers and Footers

It's pretty easy to add headers and footers, including page numbers, in Acrobat. Headers and footers take advantage of the document margins to add document information such as date, title, and page numbers.

If you select Document > Add Headers & Footers, Acrobat presents you with the Add Headers & Footers dialog box (**Figure 5.31**). This dialog box can be confusing at first, but with a bit of exploration it's quite easy to use.

Acrobat's headers and footers contain three types of information: page numbers, date, and custom text that you supply. These pieces of information may be justified at the left or right margins of the page or centered.

At the top of the dialog box are three boxes that show any information that you choose to have printed at left-justified, centered, and right-justified positions within the header or footer. Below these are a series of menus that you use to add information to each of these boxes.

To add a header or footer:

1. Choose Document > Add Headers & Footers.

   This opens the Add Headers & Footers dialog box.

2. Click the Header or Footer button at the top of the dialog box.

   The information is the same in both panes; only the final placement of the text on the page is different.

3. Click on one of the boxes at the top to choose left, center, or right alignment for your header or footer. Choose the style, page number, and font information.

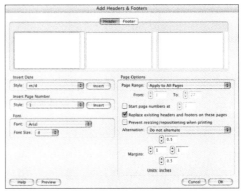

Figure 5.31 With so many settings, your header or footer can look just the way you want it to.

Figure 5.32 Click the Preview button to see how your document will look with the new header or footer before you accept it.

4. Set the style for your date and page numbering. Click the appropriate Insert button to add a date or page number. To enter custom text, select an alignment box at the top by clicking inside the box, then enter the text you want to insert.

5. In the Page Options area, use the Page Range menu to determine whether your header or footer appears on every page, alternate pages, and so on. Select margin sizes for the header or footer.

6. When you've finished adding information, you can click the Preview button to see what it will look like (**Figure 5.32**).

7. Once your header or footer looks the way you want, click OK.

✔ Tip

- To move an item from one box to another (say, from centered to right-justified), select the item in its present list and drag it to the appropriate box; you will have to delete it from the initial box. Or you can cut the text (Ctrl+X/Command+X) and paste it into the appropriate box (Ctrl+V/Command+V).

To remove and restore a header or footer:

1. Choose Edit > Undo Headers/Footers (Ctrl+Z/Command+Z) to remove a header or footer you've just added (**Figure 5.33**).

   If you've made other changes to the document since you added the header or footer, you'll have to repeat the Edit > Undo command multiple times.

2. To restore a header or footer you've just removed, choose Edit > Redo Headers/Footers (Ctrl+Shift+Z/Command+Shift+Z).

   This will put back the removed header or footer and all the information it contained. As with the Undo command, if you've restored other changes since you removed the header or footer, you'll have to use the Redo command multiple times.

To edit a header or footer:

1. Choose Document > Add Headers and Footers.

2. Click the Header or Footer tab in the dialog box. The options are the same in either tab.

3. Change any of the settings. To remove custom text, select it and click the Delete key.

✔ Tip

■ Once you save and close a PDF file, then reopen it, any headers and footers you have created become just text within the PDF file, like any other text. Among other things, this means that you can no longer edit the headers and footers in the Add Headers & Footers dialog box.

Figure 5.33 Choose Edit > Undo Headers/Footers to remove a newly minted header or footer.

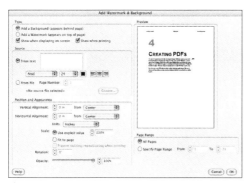

Figure 5.34 The Add Watermark & Background dialog box lets you add and position background graphics on your pages.

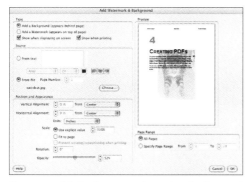

Figure 5.35 Admire the new watermark or background in the preview pane.

Working with Watermarks and Backgrounds

You can have Acrobat add a graphic or text to the background or foreground of the pages in your document. This addition can be a note, a company logo, or anything else you'd like. Acrobat calls this addition a background if it is placed behind the contents of your pages; it is a watermark if it is placed on top of your pages' contents. The source of this graphic or text is a page taken from another PDF file.

To add a watermark or background:

1. Choose Document > Add Watermark & Background.

   This opens the Add Watermark & Background dialog box (**Figure 5.34**).

2. In the Type area, choose whether to add a background or a watermark by clicking the appropriate radio button.

   Also click the check boxes to choose when to display your watermark or background: on screen, when printing, or both.

3. Click the Choose button to find the file for your watermark or background.

4. In the Open dialog box, navigate to the file you want and click Open.

   The image or text appears in the preview pane on the right of the Add Watermark & Background dialog box.

5. Select the vertical and horizontal alignment, scale, rotation, and opacity of the image.

6. Choose the pages on which you want the watermark or background displayed.

7. Preview your document in the preview pane (**Figure 5.35**). When you're happy with the effect, click OK.

✔ Tips

- The vertical and horizontal alignment let you position the background image. If you want it centered, choose Center for both vertical and horizontal alignments.

- If you have trouble seeing the text through the image, lower the opacity setting.

- Although you can apply a background to all pages or a specific page range, it's sometimes most effective to use the background for just the front page.

- To remove a watermark or background you've just added, choose Edit > Undo Add Background or Undo Add Watermark (Ctrl+Z/Command+Z). Use the Redo command (Edit > Add Background or Add Watermark or Ctrl+Shift+Z/Command+Shift+Z) to restore a watermark or background you've just removed.

- Once you save and close the PDF file, the watermark or background becomes just another set of graphic objects or text within the PDF file. You can no longer edit, remove, or otherwise manipulate it as a watermark or background.

Making PDFs Easy to Navigate

Acrobat has several features—Bookmarks, Articles, and Links—that make it easy for readers to find what they're looking for in a PDF. Many PDF authors add bookmarks to their documents to provide the reader quick access to specific passages—a capability that can be indispensable in multipage documents. You can also customize a bookmark to display a page at a certain magnification or direct the reader's attention to a specific part of the page.

Articles in Acrobat let you take a user through your document in the typical column-like style of magazines and newspaper articles. Using the Article feature makes viewing a sequential article much easier. The Article command will guide the reader through the PDF exactly the way you choose.

Links enable you to jump to other areas of the PDF document, to specific Web sites, or to a different file. You can also use links to add movies or sound clips when you're creating a multimedia PDF.

Creating Bookmarks

Bookmarks are placeholders in a document. The most helpful kind of bookmark reflects the structure of the document. Because it's possible to arrange bookmarks in hierarchies, you could construct a detailed table of contents from your bookmarks (see the bookmarks in the Acrobat Help file for a good example).

If you receive a document that contains bookmarks placed by the author, here's how to use them.

To use a bookmark:

1. Display the bookmarks pane by choosing View > Navigation tabs > Bookmarks.

   or

   Click the Bookmarks tab on the left side of the Navigation pane (**Figure 6.1**).

2. Click the bookmark you want to go to.

   The Document pane changes to show the bookmarked page.

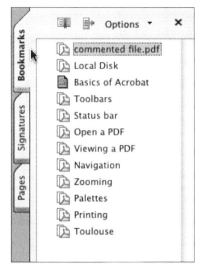

Figure 6.1 Click the tab on the left side of the window to open the Bookmarks pane.

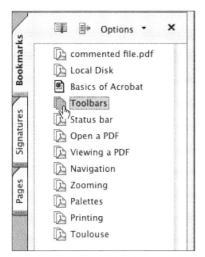

Figure 6.2 The new bookmark will be inserted after the bookmark you select in this list.

To create a bookmark:

1. In your current document, display the Bookmarks pane.

2. If your document already contains bookmarks, click to select the bookmark after which you want to add the new one (**Figure 6.2**).

3. Navigate to the spot in your document that you want to bookmark.

   This is referred to as the bookmark's *destination*.

4. Zoom in to the desired magnification at the spot on the page where you want to direct the reader's attention.

5. Use the Text Select tool to select the portion of the text that will be the bookmark.

   Make sure the text you select is descriptive enough for readers to identify the passage.

(continues on next page)

6. Click the New Bookmark button (**Figure 6.3**) at the top of the Bookmarks pane.

or

Choose New Bookmark (Ctrl+B/ Command+B) from the Options pop-up menu in the Bookmarks pane (**Figure 6.4**).

A new bookmark appears in the Bookmarks pane (**Figure 6.5**).

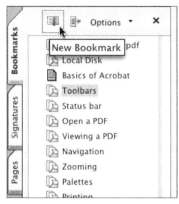

Figure 6.3 Click the New Bookmark icon at the top of the Bookmarks pane.

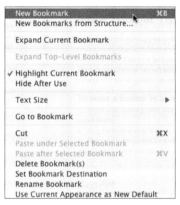

Figure 6.4 Choose New Bookmark from the Bookmarks pane's Options menu.

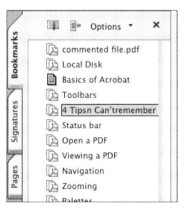

Figure 6.5 The new Bookmark will appear right where you designated it should be.

Figure 6.6 Choose Set Bookmark Destination from the Bookmarks pane's Options menu.

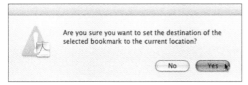

Figure 6.7 Click Yes to reset the bookmark's destination.

Moving Bookmarks

Suppose that you mistakenly created a bookmark that took the reader to the middle of a page instead of to the top. Rather than delete that bookmark and start over, you can simply change its destination.

By default, bookmarks appear in the pane in the order in which you create them. If you like, you can change that order or reorganize a long list of bookmarks into a more useful hierarchical list. For example, you may want to define one page as a main heading, or parent bookmark, and another as a subheading, or child bookmark.

To change the destination of a bookmark:

1. Open a PDF document and display the Bookmarks pane.

2. Click to select the bookmark that you want to assign a new destination.

3. Move to the new target location in the document.

4. Choose Set Bookmark Destination from the Options pop-up menu in the Bookmarks pane (**Figure 6.6**).

    A warning dialog box appears, asking if you're sure you want to change the bookmark's destination.

5. Click Yes to reset the bookmark (**Figure 6.7**).

To move a bookmark within the list:

1. Click to select the bookmark you want to move.

2. Drag the bookmark up or down in the list.

   As the mouse pointer passes over a space between two bookmarks, a dotted line appears in the space, showing you where the dragged bookmark will be placed if you release the mouse button (**Figure 6.8**).

3. Release the mouse button when you reach the desired location for the bookmark.

   The bookmark appears in its new location.

To place a bookmark beneath another in the heirarchy:

1. Click to select the bookmark you intend to define as a child.

2. Drag the bookmark until the mouse pointer is over the name of the bookmark (not the bookmark itself) that you want to define as the parent.

   A dotted line appears, showing where the dragged bookmark will be moved (**Figure 6.9**).

3. Release the mouse button.

   The dragged bookmark is now below the bookmark to which it was dragged, and that bookmark is now its parent (**Figure 6.10**). The parent bookmark is identified by a plus sign (Windows) or triangle (Mac OS) to its left. Clicking this symbol reveals the child bookmarks below the parent in the hierarchy.

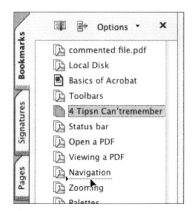

Figure 6.8 Move a bookmark by dragging it up or down in the list.

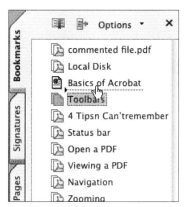

Figure 6.9 Make a child bookmark by dragging it up or down in the list.

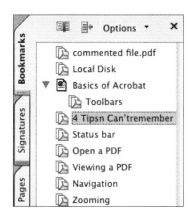

Figure 6.10 When the child bookmark is in place, it appears below the parent bookmark and is indented.

MOVING BOOKMARKS

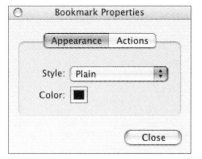

Figure 6.11 Set bookmark properties in the Bookmark Properties dialog box.

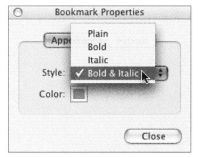

Figure 6.12 Choose a new color and style for the bookmark's name.

Changing Bookmark Properties

Reading through a long list of bookmarks can be a bit mind numbing. You can alter the appearance of bookmarks to make the hierarchy more visible and easier to navigate. For example, make all chapter headings bold and italic, and make the text for all figure references red.

To change a bookmark's properties:

1. Open the Bookmarks pane for the current document.

2. Click to select a bookmark.

3. Choose Properties from the Options pop-up menu in the Bookmarks pane. The Bookmark Properties dialog box appears (**Figure 6.11**).

4. Choose the Appearance tab.

5. To change the color or text style of the bookmark's name, click the color box or choose a style from the pop-up menu (**Figure 6.12**) in the Appearance section of the dialog box.

6. Click Close.

Creating Articles

If your document contains stories that appear on different parts of a page or span several pages, as often happens in newspapers and magazines, you can define articles within the document to guide the reader through the story from beginning to end. The Article tool lets you link the various parts of the text so that the reader will be able to follow the flow of the story.

To create an article:

1. Open the document in which you want to create the article.

2. Click the Article tool in the Advanced Editing toolbar (**Figure 6.13**).

   If the toolbar isn't visible, choose Tools > Advanced Editing > Advanced Editing Toolbar.

3. Drag the Article tool across the section of text you want to define as the first part of the article.

   When you release the mouse button, the text is numbered and surrounded by a box (**Figure 6.14**). The numbers above the box show you the article's sequence in the document and the section's sequence in the article.

4. Drag the Article tool to select the next section of text that you want to link to the first one.

   The numbering is sequential. For instance, if this section of the article is labeled 1-2, subsequent sections will be labeled 1-3, 1-4, and so on.

5. Choose View > Navigation tabs > Articles to see the Articles pane and the list of articles.

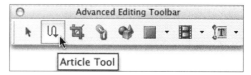

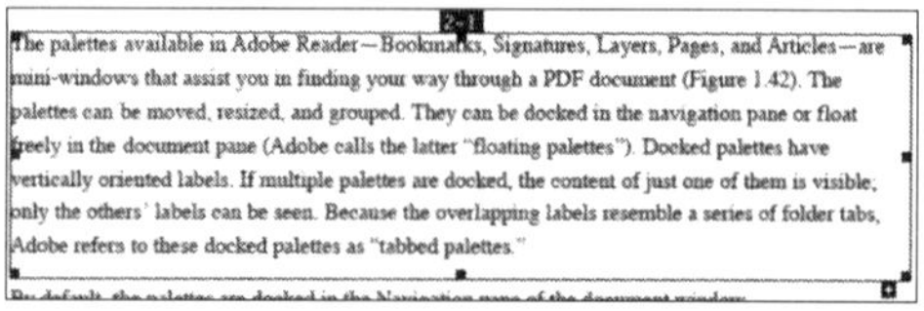

Figure 6.13 Choose the Article tool in the toolbar.

The palettes available in Adobe Reader—Bookmarks, Signatures, Layers, Pages, and Articles—are mini-windows that assist you in finding your way through a PDF document (Figure 1.42). The palettes can be moved, resized, and grouped. They can be docked in the navigation pane or float freely in the document pane (Adobe calls the latter "floating palettes"). Docked palettes have vertically oriented labels. If multiple palettes are docked, the content of just one of them is visible; only the others' labels can be seen. Because the overlapping labels resemble a series of folder tabs, Adobe refers to these docked palettes as "tabbed palettes."

Figure 6.14 The article is indicated by a box with a number above it.

Figure 6.15 After you create an article, you can use the Article Properties dialog box to add information about the article.

Figure 6.16 Drag out the corner of an article box to extend the article.

6. Double-click an article in the pane to give it a title, subject, author, and keywords in the Article Properties dialog box (**Figure 6.15**).

To extend an article:

1. Click the Article tool.

All articles in the document are displayed.

2. Click the section of the article to which you want to add material.

3. Click the plus sign in the bottom-right corner and a dialog box appears, telling you to click and drag to create a new box.

4. Click OK and drag out one or more new boxes.

The new articles boxes are appended to the existing article.

✔ Tip

■ You can also make an article box bigger so that it includes more of the page. Just click and drag on any of the handles that appear at the corners and sides of the box when you select it with the Article tool. (**Figure 6.16**).

Editing Articles

After you create articles in a PDF document, you can rename them, add or remove sections of text, combine articles into a single article, or delete articles from the document.

To rename an article:

1. Choose View > Navigation tabs > Articles to display the Articles pane.

   All the articles in the document are listed.

2. Click to select an article and choose Rename from the Options pop-up menu in the Articles pane (**Figure 6.17**).

   or

   Double-click the article's name.

3. Type a new name and then press Enter or Return.

To combine articles:

1. Click the Article tool.

2. Click the first article to be combined.

3. Click the plus sign in the bottom-right corner of the article box (**Figure 6.18**).

   Be sure to click exactly once on the small plus sign. This can be a little disconcerting, because Acrobat gives you no indication that anything special has happened when you click on the plus sign, but you should click it only once.

4. Press Ctrl (Windows) or Option (Mac OS), and click the box you want to combine with the first article (**Figure 6.19**).

   The two articles are now attached and can be read one after the other. Any other articles are renumbered.

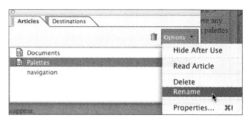

Figure 6.17 Choose Rename from the Options menu to change an article's name.

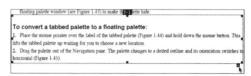

Figure 6.18 To combine articles, first click the initial portion, then click the plus sign in the bottom-right corner.

Figure 6.19 Ctrl-click or Option-click the second article to join it to the first one.

EDITING ARTICLES

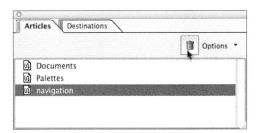

Figure 6.20 Click the Trash icon to delete selected articles.

Figure 6.21 Acrobat asks if you really want to delete the articles.

To remove an article:

1. In the Articles pane, click the article that you want to remove.

2. Click the Trash icon in the Articles pane (**Figure 6.20**).

   or

   Press Backspace or Delete.

   A dialog box appears, asking whether you're sure that you want to delete the article (**Figure 6.21**).

3. Click OK to remove the article.

Reading Articles

To read all the parts of an article from beginning to end, just follow the boxes.

To read an article:

1. Open the Articles pane.

   The Articles pane isn't visible by default; you need to select it from View > Navigation Tabs > Articles.

2. Double-click the article that you want to read.

   The cursor automatically becomes the Follow Article cursor when you double-click the article (**Figure 6.22**).

   You are taken to the start of the article.

3. Click anywhere in the article or press Enter or Return repeatedly to advance through the article; Shift-click or press Shift+Enter or Shift+Return to go backward.

   When you reach the end of the article, the mouse pointer changes to the End Article pointer. Click anywhere on the article to go back to the view you had of the document before you started to read the article.

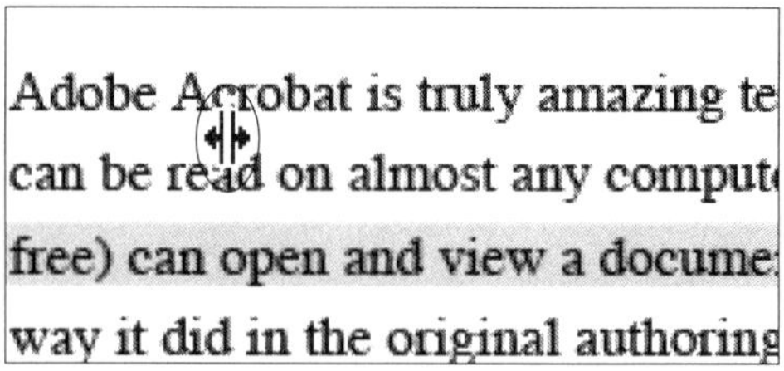

✔ Tips

- While you're reading an article, Ctrl-click or Option-click at any time to return to the start of the article.

- The hand cursor will always turn into the Follow Article cursor when it passes over an article on the page, whether or not you have the Articles pane visible.

Figure 6.22 The Follow Article pointer is displayed while you're reading an article.

Figure 6.23 Choose the Link tool from the toolbar.

Figure 6.24 Drag a rectangle around the area that will make up the link.

Figure 6.25 Choose Go to a Page View so that you can link to another page within your PDF.

Setting Links

Acrobat lets users go instantly from a particular spot in a document to nearly any other location, whether that location is on the same page, in the same document, in a different document, or even on the World Wide Web. Acrobat provides the tools to create links that give users one-click access to other locations.

Links can lead not only to other locations in PDF documents, but also (like bookmarks) to files created by other applications, to forms (which you'll learn about in Chapter 10), to JavaScript commands, to Web sites, and to multimedia files such as sound and movie clips.

Links are very easy to create using Acrobat's Link tool. Links can be obvious or hidden within the document, appearing only when the mouse pointer passes over the link.

To link one spot in a PDF document to another:

1. Open the document in which you want to create the link, and go to the page where you want to place the link.

2. Choose the Link tool from the Advanced Editing toolbar (**Figure 6.23**).

   If the Advanced Editing toolbar is not visible, choose Tools > Advanced Editing > Advanced EditingTools.

3. Drag a rectangle around the area you want to define as a link (**Figure 6.24**).

   When you release the mouse button, the Create Link dialog box appears (**Figure 6.25**). You can move this dialog box out of your way while you're setting the location of the link, but don't close it.

(continues on next page)

4. Select the Go to a Page View radio button and then click the Next button.

The Create Go to View dialog box appears and the PDF document is live behind the dialog box.

5. Use the PDF's scrollbars to navigate to the page to which you want to link. You can also zoom in on a specific spot or zoom out using the magnification tools.

6. Once you have an area on screen that you want to link to, click the Set Link button in the Create Go to View dialog box.

Acrobat sets your view back to the page that has the link button.

7. To test the link, click it with the Hand tool.

The linked-to location should appear.

Figure 6.26 You can link to another application.

✔ Tips

■ To link to a page in another document, no matter what type, click the Open a File radio button; this lets you use the Next button. Then select a file on your computer (**Figure 6.26**).

■ The Custom Link option lets the user associate a link with an action: execute a JavaScript, submit a form, and so on. For more on actions, especially on how they relate to forms, see Chapter 10.

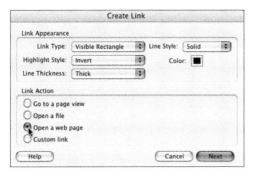

Figure 6.27 Link to the Web by choosing the Open a Web Page button in the Create Link dialog box.

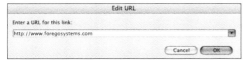

Figure 6.28 Enter a URL for the link.

Linking to the Internet

As mentioned earlier in this chapter, links can connect to locations outside Acrobat, as far as the Internet can reach. If the text of your PDF document contains URLs that you would like to act as links to the Internet, you can convert them to Web links.

To link to a Web site:

1. Open the document in which you want to create the link, and go to the page where you want to place the link.

2. Choose the Link tool from the Advanced Editing toolbar.

3. Drag a marquee around the area you want to define as a link.

   When you release the mouse button, the Create Link dialog box appears.

4. Click the Open a Web Page radio button in the Create Link dialog box (**Figure 6.27**).

5. Click the Next button and the Edit URL dialog box appears. In the Address field, type the URL of the Web site to which you want to link (**Figure 6.28**) and click OK.

To convert multiple URLs to Web links automatically:

1. Choose Advanced > Links > Create from URLs in Document (**Figure 6.29**).

   The Create Web Links dialog box opens (**Figure 6.30**).

2. Choose whether to generate links on all pages or in a range of pages.

   Acrobat sifts through the pages you specify, searching for URLs, which it converts to Web links. Unfortunately, this process will often miss URLs in the text, so you should go through and make sure all the links were successfully created.

✔ Tips

- The Web links are invisible initially. To find them, choose the Link tool from the Advanced Editing toolbar; then select each Web link to set its properties (see the following step-by-step procedure for details).

- URLs must be contained within a single line of text for the command to find them. They must also include the protocol prefix (such as `http://` or `ftp://`) to be recognized as URLs.

To set the properties of a Web link:

1. Using the Link tool, select a Web link (**Figure 6.31**).

2. Right-click/Control-click to activate the contextual menu.

3. Choose Properties (**Figure 6.32**).

   The Link Properties dialog box appears.

4. To change the appearance of the Web link, click the Appearance tab and select Visible Rectangle from the Link Type, or make any other changes you want.

5. Click the Close button to accept these changes (**Figure 6.33**).

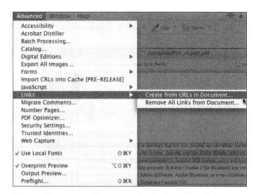

Figure 6.29 Turn all your text URLs into Web links.

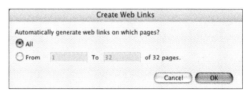

Figure 6.30 Which pages do you want to contain links to the Web?

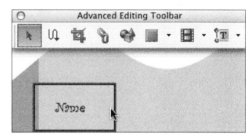

Figure 6.31 The outline of the link appears when you click on the link with the Link tool.

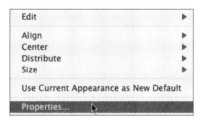

Figure 6.32 To access the Link Properties dialog box, select Properties from the contextual menu.

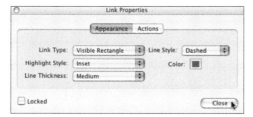

Figure 6.33 The changes will show after you click the Close button.

Figure 6.34 Make your link look like a button.

Figure 6.35 Choose how you want to open a Web link.

To set a link's appearance:

1. With the Link tool, right-click/Control-click the link and choose Properties from the contextual menu.

   This brings up the link's Properties dialog box.

2. Choose Visible Rectangle from the Link Type pop-up menu.

3. Choose Inset from the Highlight Style pop-up menu.

4. Click the Close button to activate these settings.

   Use the Hand tool to see the link, which now looks something like a button (**Figure 6.34**).

To activate a Web link:

1. Open the document containing the links.

2. Using the Hand tool, click the Web link.

   The first time you click any Web link, you'll see the Specify Weblink Behavior dialog box (**Figure 6.35**).

3. Specify whether you want to open Web links in Acrobat or in your Web browser.

   If you choose the In Acrobat radio button, Acrobat attempts to download the Web pages at the URL, convert them to PDF, and append them to the current document. If you choose the In Web Browser radio button, your default browser will open and display the Web page when the link is clicked. It's safer to choose Web Browser so that you don't find yourself adding thousands of pages to your document.

✔ Tip

■ Set Web Capture preferences by choosing Edit (Acrobat in Mac OS X) > Preferences > Web Capture.

Editing Links

After you set a link, you may decide that it should have a different appearance or should perform a different action. And of course, if it's a Web link, it's quite likely (given the fluid nature of the Web) that the site will change or disappear at some point. Fortunately, editing or deleting a link is as easy as setting it up.

To edit an existing link:

1. With the document open to the page that contains the link, choose the Link tool from the Advanced Editing toolbar.

2. Double-click an existing link.

   or

   Right-click/Control-click the link and choose Properties from the contextual menu.

   The outline of the link is displayed along with the Link Properties dialog box (**Figure 6.36**).

3. Change options using the pop-up menus in the Appearance tab or the Actions tab (**Figure 6.37**).

   In the Actions tab, click the Open a Web Link with the URL you want to change, and then choose the Edit button. This brings up the Edit URL dialog box (**Figure 6.38**). Enter a new address and click OK, then close the Properties dialog box for the changes to take effect.

   In the Appearance section, choose the appearance you want your link to have, whether a rectangle that stands out from the surrounding text, or no distinguishing features whatsoever.

   In the Actions tab you can select Open a Web Link, Go to a Page, Play a Sound, and Submit a Form, among other actions.

4. Click OK to set the link changes.

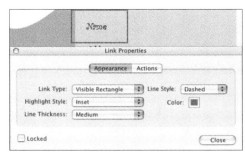

Figure 6.36 The outline of the link appears, along with the Link Properties dialog box.

Figure 6.37 Alter the appearance or actions of the link by using the Link Properties dialog box.

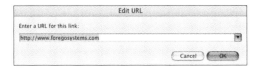

Figure 6.38 You can change the URL you had assigned to the link.

EDITING LINKS

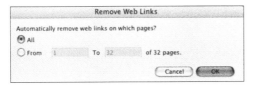

Figure 6.39 Acrobat double-checks with you before removing your Web links.

To delete a link:

1. Choose the Link tool from the Advanced Editing toolbox.

2. Click the link you want to delete.
   The outline of the link is displayed.

3. Press the Backspace or Delete key.
   or
   Choose Edit > Delete.
   The link is removed.

To delete all Web links:

1. Choose Advanced > Links > Remove All Web Links from Document.
   The Remove Web Links dialog box appears (**Figure 6.39**).

2. Specify whether to delete Web links from all pages or a range of pages.

3. Click OK.

Add a Link for Downloading Acrobat Reader

If you want visitors to your Web site to be able to download Adobe Reader 6 so they can read your PDF documents, you can install a link to Adobe that starts a download of Reader. Follow these steps:

1. In your HTML editor, type this line:

   `<A HREF = "http://www.adobe.com/products/acrobat/readstep2.html">`

2. On the next line, type the words that you want to use as the link, such as the following:

   `Click here to download Adobe Reader`

3. On the last line, type </A> to tell the browser that it has reached the end of the hyper-linked text.

ADDING
COMMENTS

7

Acrobat ships with a variety of tools that you can use to mark up PDF documents. Using these tools, you can highlight and underline text as well as include notes, stamps, file attachments, and sound comments.

You can use comments to request changes in a document or to call attention to important areas. Acrobat lets you filter out the comments you don't want to see so that only the markings relevant to you appear. You can also create a document that summarizes all the comments made in a document.

Comments in PDFs are the heart of reviewing documents in a work group. Upcoming chapters will show how to manage comments and provide information on working on a review cycle. For now, we'll review the basics of adding comments.

Understanding Types of Comments

You can access the Commenting toolbar (**Figure 7.1**) from the View > Toolbars > Commenting submenu. Acrobat offers several types of comments, each designed for a specific type of task:

- The **Note tool** lets you create collapsible text boxes in which you can include information about a specific area in a document (**Figure 7.2**).

- **Text Edits** are comments applied directly to the text of a PDF, including everything from inserting text and notes to highlighting and underlining (**Figure 7.3**). You'll find all the text editing features, such as replacing, highlighting, and inserting text, in their own pull-down menu in the Commenting toolbar.

- **Drawing Markup Tools** (View > Toolbars > Drawing Markups) are tools that let you mark up your PDF with callouts, lines, shapes, rectangles, and circles (**Figure 7.4**). Choose from a variety of standard shapes or choose the Pencil tool to create your own freeform shape. New to Acrobat 7 is the Dimensioning tool, which lets you add dimension lines to your PDF document and then use the Callout tool to add the actual dimension numbers to the dimension line. The Drawing Markup tools are geared toward engineering users. For example, an AutoCAD image turned into a PDF would benefit from someone using the Drawing Markup tools to add to a review process.

Figure 7.1 The Commenting toolbar holds most of the tools you'll use for adding comments to documents.

Figure 7.2 An expanded note is a good place to write detailed information about a specific area of a PDF document.

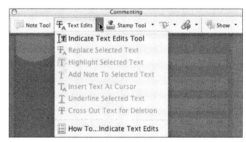

Figure 7.3 Text Edits lets you mark the document directly without having to open a note.

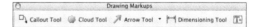

Figure 7.4 You can choose from a variety of Drawing Markup tools.

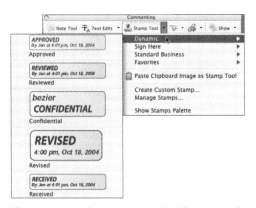

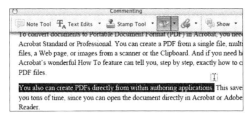

Figure 7.5 A sample stamp annotation. The Approved stamp indicates that your PDF is final.

Figure 7.6 The Highlight tool highlights areas of text.

Figure 7.7 Choose Commenting Preferences from the Show menu to change the default Commenting preferences.

◆ **Stamps** are graphics that can be applied to any page of a document (**Figure 7.5**). For example, you can use a stamp to show that a document has been reviewed and approved by you. You can also create custom stamps.

◆ **Highlights** apply certain effects to the selected text, including underline, strikethrough, and, of course, highlight (**Figure 7.6**). Most of these effects are also available under the Text Edits menu, but it's quicker to apply them directly from the Commenting toolbar.

◆ **Attach File as a Comment** is a useful set of tools if you need to include more information than will fit in a note or text box, such as a source file or a file that contains updated or corrected information. Sound attachments are files that contain recorded audio; they add a sound to a specific area of a PDF file.

◆ **Show** lets you see a reviewer's comments on a PDF file. Choose Comments List from the Show pull-down menu and a Comments List pane appears at the bottom of your document. You can choose to sort the comments by a number of criteria, including comment type, reviewer, or status. You can set your Commenting preferences by choosing Show > Commenting Preferences (**Figure 7.7**).

To change a comment's properties, right-click/Control-click the icon and then choose Properties from the contextual menu. To remove comments, use the Hand tool to select the comment and then press Backspace/Delete.

Enabling Reader Users to Add Comments

New to Acrobat 7 Professional is the ability to enable users of Adobe Reader to add comments to your PDF. Let's say you have a PDF you want to get some feedback on and you need to send it to several people. Everyone may not have Acrobat Professional, but anyone can get a copy of Adobe Reader 7.0 since it's free. Acrobat's new ability makes it possible to collaborate with those users who don't have Acrobat but do have Reader.

Figure 7.8 You can enable for commenting in Adobe Reader 7.0.

To enable a PDF for commenting in Reader

1. Open the document that you want to enable for Reader.

2. Choose Comments > Enable For Commenting in Adobe Reader (**Figure 7.8**).

   This launches the Reader Enable Document for Commenting dialog box, which warns you that once you enable the document, it will become restricted for all users, even those using Acrobat.

Figure 7.9 Acknowledge the restrictions that enabling commenting in Reader will have on your PDF in Acrobat.

3. Click the OK button (**Figure 7.9**).

   The Save As dialog box launches for you to give the file a new name or overwrite the old one.

4. Enter a name for the file and click Save.

✔ Tip

■ Access the Send by Email for Review wizard by choosing Comments > Send for Review > Send by Email for Review. Use the Send by Email for Review wizard to set up a reviewing process, including people with free Adobe Reader. In the second step, click Customize Review Options to check the Also Allow Users of Free Adobe Reader 7.0 to Participate box.

Figure 7.10 Choose the Note tool from the Commenting toolbar.

Figure 7.11 A note of default size is created when you just click.

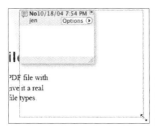

Figure 7.12 Click and drag to create a note any size you'd like.

Figure 7.13 Close the note by clicking in the box in the note's upper-right corner.

Figure 7.14 The note icon remains visible in the document.

Creating and Editing Notes

Notes are the most basic and common form of comments. Think of them as notes that you can stick onto your documents. You can use notes to keep track of changes or to indicate changes you'd like to see in the text without actually making them. Because you can choose (in the Print dialog box) to have notes hidden in the printed document, you can also use them to add information that's hidden from the public.

To create a note:

1. With a document open, choose the Note tool (**Figure 7.10**) from the Commenting toolbar.

2. Place the note by clicking the document page where you want the note icon to be shown.

   A note appears in the default size, with the name of the note's author and the date and time at the top (**Figure 7.11**).

   If you'd like to change the size of the note box, click the lower-right corner with the Hand tool and drag to the desired size (**Figure 7.12**).

3. Type your note in the box.

4. Click the close box in the top-right corner of the note to close the note when you've finished entering text (**Figure 7.13**).

   A note icon remains in the document at the spot you clicked to create the note (**Figure 7.14**).

To edit an existing note:

1. Double-click the note icon to expand the note.

2. Click in the existing text to place the insertion point at the desired location (**Figure 7.15**).

3. Edit the text as desired, including cutting or copying text or pasting it from another location.

✔ Tip

■ You can edit or delete notes while the Hand tool is selected.

To set the font and size of the text in a note:

1. Choose Edit > Preferences > General (Ctrl-K/Command-K) to open the Preferences dialog box.

2. Select Commenting in the list of categories on the left side of the dialog box (**Figure 7.16**).

3. Choose the font size from the pop-up menus, and set the opacity of the note boxes and the behavior of various types of comments.

To change the color of a note:

1. Right-click/Control-click the note icon and then choose Properties from the contextual menu (**Figure 7.17**). You can also choose Properties from the Options arrow in the note.

   The Note Properties dialog box opens.

2. Click the Appearance tab.

3. Click the Color button (**Figure 7.18**) to select a standard color.

   or

Figure 7.15 Place your mouse cursor where you want to insert the text.

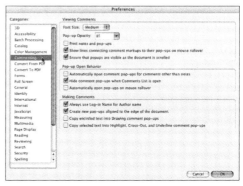

Figure 7.16 Select Commenting in the list on the left to change the preferences for comments.

Figure 7.17 Right-click/Control-click to access the contextual menu for Properties.

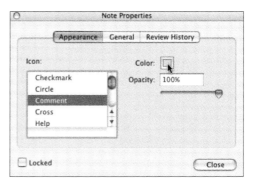

Figure 7.18 Click the Color button.

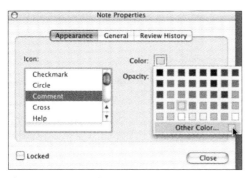

Figure 7.19 Select Other Color to access your system's color picker.

Figure 7.20 If you use a Mac, the dialog box for your color picker might look like this.

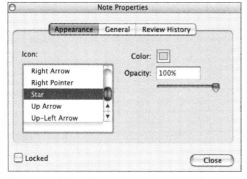

Figure 7.21 Select the note icon you want in the Note Properties dialog box. You can see the new note icon when you click on the document.

Choose Other Color at the bottom (**Figure 7.19**).

This brings up your system's color picker dialog box (**Figure 7.20**).

4. Choose a different color, and click OK to close the Color Picker.

5. Click Close in the Properties dialog box to change the note's color.

✔ Tip

■ To move a note, choose a different tool (such as the Hand tool), click on the note, and drag it to a new location.

To change the note icon:

1. Right-click/Control-click the note icon and then choose Properties from the contextual menu. You can also choose Properties from the Options arrow in the note.

   The Note Properties dialog box opens.

2. Click the Appearance tab.

3. Under the Icon list, choose a different icon for your note. Choose from a variety of icons. To see your new icon, click on it and look at the document (**Figure 7.21**).

Using Text Edits

Text comments provide another method of adding and editing text in a document. More immediately visible than notes, text comments display the text directly in the document. These are the text editing options:

♦ **Indicate Text Edits** selects the text to which you want to apply an edit. Drag the cursor across the text you want to select.

♦ **Replace Selected Text** will automatically cross out the selected text, insert a caret, and open a box for inserting text (**Figure 7.22**).

♦ **Highlight Selected Text** essentially does the same as the Highlighter tool: Once you select the text and choose Highlight Selected Text, the text will be highlighted.

♦ **Add Note to Selected Text** automatically highlights the text and opens a Comment on Text box (**Figure 7.23**).

♦ **Insert Text at Cursor** inserts a caret at the selected point for you to insert text. The text will be inserted in a note box.

♦ **Underline Selected Text** does the same as the Underline Text tool.

♦ **Cross Out Text for Deletion** does the same as the Cross-Out Text tool. It will cross out the selected text indicating the deletion.

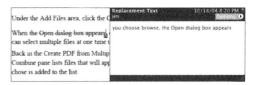

Figure 7.22 Replace the selected text by adding new text in the box.

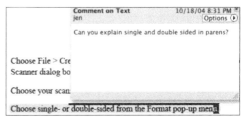

Figure 7.23 Add a note to the selected text.

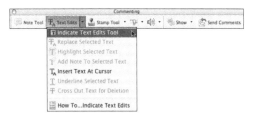

Figure 7.24 To start editing text, choose the Indicate Text Edits tool.

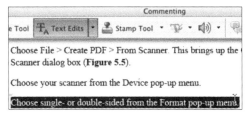

Figure 7.25 Drag to select the section of text you want to edit.

Figure 7.26 The caret marks where the new text should be inserted.

Figure 7.27 It's easy to replace text wherever you need to.

To create a text edit:

1. Click the arrow next to Text Edits in the Commenting toolbar and choose the Indicate Text Edits tool (**Figure 7.24**).

2. Drag to select the text that you want to edit (**Figure 7.25**).

3. Choose an edit function from the Text Edits menu.

   The edit you choose will affect the selected text.

To insert text:

1. With the Indicate Text Edits tool, click where you want to insert text.

2. Choose the Insert Text at Cursor tool. This will automatically insert a caret in the text and open a blue Inserted Text note box (**Figure 7.26**).

3. In the note box, type the text you want to insert.

4. Close the note by clicking the close box in the top-right corner.

To replace text:

1. With the Indicate Text Edits tool, select the text you want to replace.

2. Choose the Replace Selected Text tool and the text you selected will automatically be crossed out, a caret will be inserted, and a blue note box for inserting text will open (**Figure 7.27**).

3. Enter the text you want to be inserted into the note.

4. Close the note by clicking the close box in the top corner of the note box.

USING TEXT EDITS

To change the properties of text edits:

1. Right-click/Control-click the text edit and then choose Properties from the contextual menu.

   The Properties dialog box for that edit type appears (**Figure 7.28**).

2. Change any of the options.

3. Click Close.

✔ Tip

■ The Appearance tab lets you change such properties as the color and opacity. The General tab lists the author, type of text edit, and date. The last tab lists the Review History and any changes to the comment. Although the Appearance tab options change depending on the type of edit that's selected, the latter two tabs are always the same.

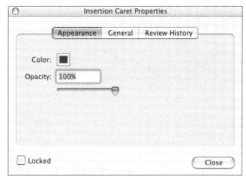

Figure 7.28 The Properties dialog box lets you change options for the selected editing tool.

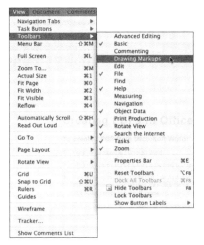

Figure 7.29 The Text Box tool is under the Drawing Markups toolbar.

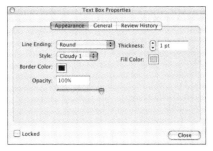

Figure 7.30 Type your comment at the blinking cursor.

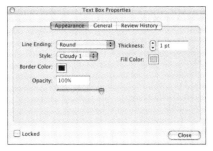

Figure 7.31 Change settings in the Text Box Properties dialog box.

Using the Text Box Tool

Starting with Version 6.0 of Acrobat you have been able to add comments directly to a page using the Text Box tool. Most text edits done with other editing tools show up as a high-light, strikethrough, or icon, plus a comment in a pop-up window; the Text Box tool's comments are right there on the page. It's like writing right on a paper document, as opposed to adding a sticky note to the paper. Double-click a text box to edit its properties.

To use the Text Box tool:

1. Select the Text Box tool in the Drawing Markups toolbar. If the toolbar isn't showing, choose View > Toolbars > Drawing Markups (**Figure 7.29**).

2. Click and drag a box out to the desired size.

3. Type your comment (**Figure 7.30**).

To change the properties of a text box:

1. Right-click/Control-click the text box to activate the contextual menu.

2. Choose Properties.

3. Make your changes in the Text Box Properties dialog box (**Figure 7.31**).
   You can change the line ending, line style, border color, opacity, thickness (in points), and fill color of the box. As you change the properties, the box simultaneously changes in the document.

4. Click the Close button.

Using Audio Attachments

To add spoken commentary (or a musical interlude, if the document calls for it) to a PDF document, use an audio attachment. If your computer has a microphone or you have sounds on your system already, you can easily add sound to a PDF.

To attach a sound file to a document:

1. Choose Record Audio Comment from the Commenting toolbar (**Figure 7.32**).

2. Choose the spot where the sound attachment will go by clicking the document page.

   The Record Sound dialog box appears (**Figure 7.33**).

3. Click the Choose button to bring up the Select Sound File dialog box and access the sounds on your computer.

4. Navigate to the sound that you want to use and click the Select button (**Figure 7.34**).

   You can choose from WAV and AIFF sound attachments.

5. To hear the sound, click the Play button, then click the OK button.

   The Sound Attachment Properties dialog box opens automatically, in case you want to make any changes (**Figure 7.35**).

Figure 7.32 Choose the Record Audio Comment tool from the pop-up menu under the File Attachment tool in the Commenting toolbar.

Figure 7.33 Choose or record a sound in the Record Sound dialog box.

Figure 7.34 Choose a sound on your system.

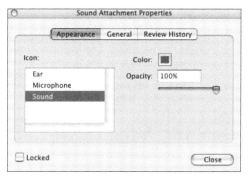

Figure 7.35 Use the Sound Attachment Properties dialog box to make any changes.

Figure 7.36 An icon appears where you attached your sound.

Figure 7.37 Click Record to record your audio comment.

Figure 7.38 Click Stop to finish the recording.

6. Click the Close button to dismiss this dialog box.

An icon appears on the page where your attachment was placed (**Figure 7.36**).

Double-click the sound attachment icon to play the sound.

✔ Tip

- Be aware that attaching even a short sound can greatly increase the size of your PDF file, so make sure it's worth the extra kilobytes.

Use the Record button to add an audio comment to a PDF document. This adds a more personal touch to your comments on the PDF file.

To record your own sound for a document:

1. Choose Record Audio Comment from the Commenting toolbar.

2. Place the sound attachment by clicking the document page.

The Record Sound dialog box appears.

3. Click the Record button to record your comment (**Figure 7.37**).

Although you will see no indication onscreen that Acrobat is recording, your microphone is now live. Start speaking or otherwise making your recorded comment.

4. Click the Stop button to stop recording your comment (**Figure 7.38**).

The Sound Attachment Properties dialog box opens automatically, in case you want to make any changes.

5. Click the Close button to dismiss this dialog box.

An icon appears on the page where your attachment was placed.

6. Double-click the sound attachment icon to play the sound.

Stamping PDFs

My favorite commenting feature is the Stamp tool, which allows you to place stamps anywhere in a document. You can stamp a document as Confidential, Top Secret, Working Draft, or For Your Eyes Only. You can even add custom stamps; any graphic file saved as a PDF can be placed as a custom stamp. Several stamp categories are built in:

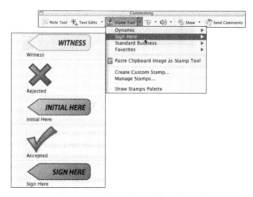

Figure 7.39 Choose a stamp from the categories under the Stamp tool.

◆ **Dynamic** stamps include information on when and by whom a stamp was applied.

◆ **The Sign Here** stamp choices are Rejected, Accepted, Initial Here, Sign Here, and Witness.

◆ **Standard Business** stamps include Approved, Completed, Confidential, Draft, Final, Not Approved, Not for Public Release, and Void.

Figure 7.40 Your stamp appears on your document. You can resize it by dragging any of the corners.

◆ **Favorites** lets you organize the comments you use most frequently.

To add a stamp to a document:

1. From the pop-up menu under the Stamp tool, choose a category submenu and select the stamp you want to use (**Figure 7.39**).

   Next to the name, you can see a preview of the stamp you've chosen.

2. Click in the document or drag over an area that matches the size of the stamp you chose as closely as possible (you can always resize it later).

   A stamp appears (**Figure 7.40**).

STAMPING PDFs

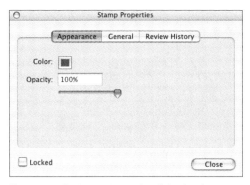

Figure 7.41 The Stamp Properties dialog box lets you change some options for the stamp.

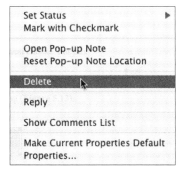

Figure 7.42 Choose Delete from the contextual menu.

3. Right-click/Control-click the stamp and select Properties from the contextual menu.

The Stamp Properties dialog box appears (**Figure 7.41**).

4. Change any of the stamp's properties (color and opacity of the note attached with the stamp), then click OK.

✔ Tip

■ When you select the Stamp tool again, the active stamp will be the last one you selected. You can always change the stamp by choosing another from the menu.

To remove a stamp from a document:

◆ Click the stamp to select it and then press Backspace/Delete.

or

Right-click/Control-click the stamp and then choose Delete from the contextual menu (**Figure 7.42**).

STAMPING PDFS

Creating Custom Stamps

You can use any graphic program that can save a file as a PDF to create custom stamps for Acrobat. You'll get the best results, however, if you create the graphic in a vector-based program such as Adobe Illustrator, because you'll be able to resize the stamp and keep the clean vector lines, rather than getting pixilated (rough, bumpy) edges. Because Acrobat treats PDF documents as containers for stamps, you can export an Illustrator document as a PDF page and use that "page" as a stamp. Acrobat knows enough to discard the white space around the graphic, so only the content area of the page will become the new stamp.

Figure 7.43 Here's the Illustrator artwork I've created to use as a custom stamp within Acrobat.

To create a custom stamp in Illustrator and Acrobat:

1. In Adobe Illustrator, create the artwork you want to use as a stamp (**Figure 7.43**).

2. Choose Save As from the File menu. The Save As dialog box appears (**Figure 7.44**).

3. Choose Acrobat PDF from the Format pop-up menu (**Figure 7.45**). This brings up the Adobe PDF Format Options dialog box. Choose your settings and click OK.

4. In the Save As dialog box, choose a save location and click OK to save your artwork as a PDF.

Figure 7.44 When I save the file, I give it a name—pigstamp—that tells me what to look for within Acrobat.

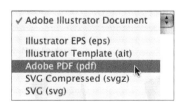

Figure 7.45 Choose a format from the pop-up menue at the bottom of the Save As dialog box.

CREATING CUSTOM STAMPS

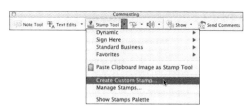

Figure 7.46 Choose Create Custom Stamp from the Stamp tool's pop-up menu.

5. In Acrobat, choose Create Custom Stamp from the Stamp tool pop-up menu (**Figure 7.46**).

This brings up the Select Image for Custom Stamp dialog box (**Figure 7.47**).

6. Click the Browse button to bring up the Open dialog box (**Figure 7.48**).

(continues on next page)

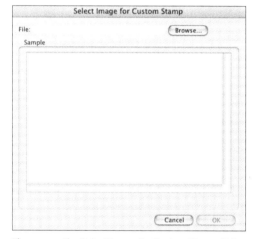

Figure 7.47 The Select Image for Custom Stamp dialog box lets you find the stamp and name it.

Figure 7.48 Find your stamp using the Open dialog box.

7. Navigate to the file and click the Select button (**Figure 7.49**). This takes you back to the Select dialog box, which should now display the stamp and the location. Click the OK button to return to the Create Custom Stamp dialog box.

You'll now see the stamp in the Create Custom Stamp dialog box.

9. Enter a category and a name for the new stamp, then click OK (**Figure 7.50**).

10. Choose the new stamp from the Stamp tool menu (**Figure 7.51**).

11. Drag out your new stamp to the size you'd like (**Figure 7.52**).

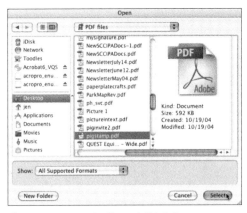

Figure 7.49 Locate the file and click Select.

Figure 7.50 The stamp you created will show in the Create Custom Stamp dialog box.

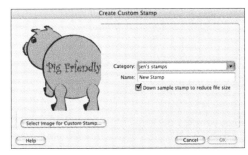

Figure 7.51 Choose the new stamp from the submenu for the category you specified.

Figure 7.52 Place the new stamp and drag it out to the size you'd like.

Figure 7.53 Add or delete stamps in the Manage Custom Stamps dialog box.

✔ Tip

■ To remove any custom stamps, choose Manage Stamps from the Stamp menu. In the Manage Custom Stamps dialog box (**Figure 7.53**), you can add or delete any stamps you've created, add categories for organizing your stamps, and change your stamp categories. You can also add your stamp to your Favorites list. Use the Downsample stamp to reduce file size option when you are working with any custom stamps using pixel-based images. If you are using a basic custom stamp, such as one using text or line art, then you don't need to use this new feature.

CREATING CUSTOM STAMPS

Creating a File Attachment

You can attach any type of file to a PDF document using the Advanced Commenting toolbar. It could be an image, a spreadsheet, or another PDF file. In some cases, you might even want to attach the non-PDF source file to the PDF document.

Figure 7.54 Choose the Attach a File as a Comment tool.

To attach another file to a PDF document:

1. With a document open, choose Attach a File as a Comment from the Commenting toolbar (**Figure 7.54**).

2. Click in the PDF document where you'd like to attach the file.

   The Add Attachment dialog box appears (**Figure 7.55**).

Figure 7.55 The Add Attachment dialog box opens so you can choose the right file.

3. Navigate to the file you want to attach, and click Select.

   The File Attachment Properties dialog box appears (**Figure 7.56**).

4. In the Appearance tab, select the icon you would like to use, and its opacity and color.

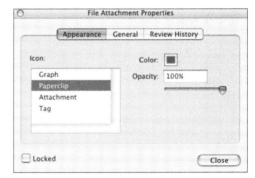

Figure 7.56 Select the icon you prefer in the File Attachment Properties dialog box.

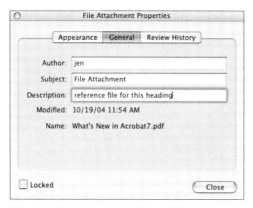

Figure 7.57 Enter any description you'd like in the General pane.

5. If you like, type a description and other information in the General tab (**Figure 7.57**).

6. Click Close.

   The file is attached to the document. When you click the Attach file icon (which can be a paperclip, graph, push pin, or a tag), the attached file will open.

✔ Tip

- When you attach a file to a PDF document, you are embedding that file within the document and dramatically increasing its size. If the file you're attaching is a large one, you might have the option of converting it to a PDF and adding those pages to the existing PDF, then linking to the additional pages. In many cases, though, a file you would have attached to a PDF, such as a source document, won't work well as a PDF, so you must make the file-size decision.

ADVANCED
COMMENTING

Commenting on a PDF file can go beyond applying a note or altering text. With the Advanced Commenting and Drawing Markups tools, you can add shapes, lines, callouts, and dimension lines.

Design professionals will appreciate using the scaling and pasting tools to arrange a PDF just as they want. Engineers will delight in the ability to use the Snap To feature to move objects to a specific point.

Editing with the Drawing Markups Tools

Use the drawing tools as you would use a pencil or pen to mark up a PDF page and to show the areas you want to edit. The drawing tools let you draw specific shapes around sections of text, point to areas in a PDF, and explain comments in a PDF.

- The **Callout** tool creates a note with an arrow to point to a specific area in your document (**Figure 8.1**).

- The **Cloud** tool works just like the polygon tool in how it draws a shape. When the shape is completed, it looks like a cloud (**Figure 8.2**).

- The **drawing** tools in the Drawing Markups toolbar let you use graphic objects as comments. You can create arrows, rectangles, ovals, lines, polygons, and polygon lines to illustrate your point (**Figure 8.3**). Use the Pencil tool to draw a free-form shape and the Pencil Eraser tool to erase any parts of your Pencil-drawn line.

- The **Dimensioning** tool draws dimension lines at points you select (**Figure 8.4**).

- **Text Box** comments is not in the Drawing Markups toolbar, but is so closely related to the functions in that toolbar that it warrants including in this list. Text Box comments is in the Advanced Commenting toolbar and it allows you to add text in a box to the document, like putting a sticky note right on the document. It doesn't collapse like a note does, and you can jazz up the box the note is in. You can access the properties of the text box to change the font, box color, and other options. For more on using the Text Box tool, see Chapter 7.

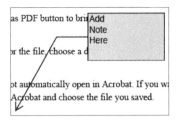

Figure 8.1 The Callout tool makes a note with a pointing arrow.

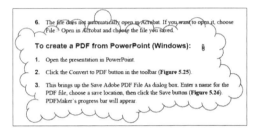

Figure 8.2 The Cloud tool lets you draw cloud-like shapes around areas of your PDF.

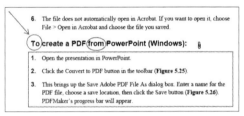

Figure 8.3 Use the Drawing tools to make a visual point.

Figure 8.4 The Dimensioning tool lets you create dimension lines.

Figure 8.5 Choose the drawing tool you want to use from the Drawing Markups toolbar under the Arrow tool.

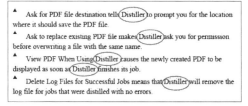

Figure 8.6 Use the drawing tools to mark up the PDF.

Figure 8.7 The Pencil tool is in the Arrow Tool menu.

Figure 8.8 Use the Pencil tool to draw a free-form shape.

Figure 8.9 The Pencil Eraser tool removes the line created by the Pencil tool.

To mark up a page with the drawing tools:

1. Select the tool you want to use from the Drawing Markups toolbar (**Figure 8.5**).

2. Click or drag in the document page to draw with the tool you've selected on the PDF document (**Figure 8.6**).

✔ Tips

■ You can change the size of the shape you created by selecting the shape with the Hand tool. Adjustment handles appear on the shape, and you can drag them out (to make them larger) or in (to make them smaller). As you drag the box corner, hold the Shift key to preserve the proportions of the shape.

■ Hold down the Shift key to constrain your lines to 45-degree angles, your ellipses to circles, and your rectangles to squares. The Shift key has no effect on the Pencil tool.

To use the Pencil tool:

1. Select the Pencil tool from the Drawing Markups toolbar (**Figure 8.7**).

2. Draw a free-form shape with the Pencil tool (**Figure 8.8**).

3. Click with the Hand tool to deselect the shape.

To use the Pencil Eraser tool:

1. Select the Pencil Eraser tool from the Drawing Markups toolbar.

2. Click the shape to erase small sections of the path. You can also just drag the tool across any part of the pencil line you want to delete (**Figure 8.9**).

To change the line weight and color:

1. With the Hand tool, right-click/Control-click the edge of the line you have drawn.

2. Choose Properties from the contextual menu.

   The Properties dialog box for the selected shape appears (**Figure 8.10**).

3. Click on the Appearance tab. In the Thickness field, type a new value or click the up and down arrows to change the thickness.

   You'll see the changes immediately on the selected line.

4. Make selections for color and opacity, if desired.

   The changes take effect immediately (**Figure 8.11**).

5. Click Close in the Properties dialog box.

✔ Tip

■ With the Rectangle, Polygon, and Oval tools, you can also choose different border and fill colors.

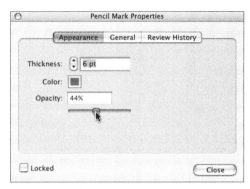

Figure 8.10 In this Properties dialog box, you can change the appearance of the line.

Figure 8.11 The changes in the Properties dialog box take immediate effect.

Figure 8.12 You can edit text with the TouchUp Text tool.

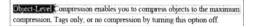

Figure 8.13 Drag across the text to select it.

Editing Text

Another way to edit a document is to actually change the text, not just comment on it. You can change any text in Acrobat with the TouchUp Text tool in the Advanced Editing toolbar. Unlike the Select Text tool, TouchUp Text enables you to change the text. One important caveat is that you must have the same font installed on your system as the text that you wish to change. Acrobat will let you know if this condition is not met.

To use the TouchUp Text tool:

1. Select the TouchUp Text tool in the Advanced Editing toolbar (**Figure 8.12**).

2. Click any line of text in the PDF document.

   A box appears around the line of text.

3. Select text within the box by dragging across it (**Figure 8.13**).

4. Replace the selected text by typing, or delete it by pressing the Backspace/ Delete key.

You can also use the TouchUp Text tool to adjust the typographical attributes of a line of text, such as the style or size of text.

To edit text attributes:

1. Select the TouchUp Text tool in the Advanced Editing toolbar.

2. Click anywhere within the line of text you want to change.

   A box appears around the line.

3. Right-click/Control-click the text, then choose Properties from the contextual menu to access the TouchUp Properties dialog box.

(continues on next page)

EDITING TEXT

The dialog box (**Figure 8.14**) lists the following options:

◆ **Font** lists all fonts installed on your system. (If you want to see the fonts in the document, choose Document Properties and click the Font tab.)

◆ **Font Size** lets you choose text size from 6-point to 72-point type.

◆ **Character Spacing** lets you adjust the spacing between two or more characters.

◆ **Word Spacing** lets you adjust the spacing between two or more words.

◆ **Horizontal Scaling** sets the ratio between the width and the height of the type. Change the Horizontal scale to jazz up the look of a heading by making it wider to fit across a page.

◆ **Embed** lets you specify whether to embed the font in the PDF.

◆ **Subset** lets you create a super- or subscript text.

◆ **Fill Color** and **Stroke** let you change the color of the selected text.

◆ **Stroke Width** lets you enter a stroke weight in points for the selected text. In other words, you choose the weight of the line around each individual letter.

◆ **Baseline Offset** sets the text's vertical offset from the baseline (also known as superscript or subscript style).

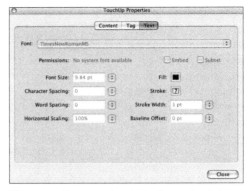

Figure 8.14 Choose options in the Properties dialog box to change the text's font, size, and more.

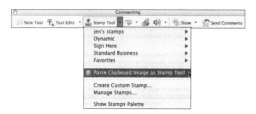

Figure 8.15 Use a Clipboard image to make a stamp.

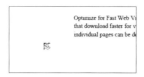

Figure 8.16 Decide where you want to place your image.

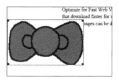

Figure 8.17 When you click with the Stamp tool, the image appears on your PDF.

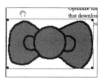

Figure 8.18 Use the Hand tool to select your stamped image.

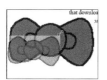

Figure 8.19 Click and drag the corners to resize your image.

Paste Clipboard Image

New to Acrobat 7 is the ability to paste a copied image from the Clipboard. Using the Stamp tool, you can add images easily to your PDF. Use any Clipboard image to create a new stamp. Then with the Stamp tool, add the images and resize as you wish.

To paste a Clipboard image into a stamp:

1. Select the Paste Clipboard Image as Stamp Tool under the Stamp tool in the Commenting toolbar (**Figure 8.15**).

2. Place the Stamp tool where you want the image to be (**Figure 8.16**).

3. Click to place the image on the PDF document (**Figure 8.17**).

To resize a Clipboard image:

1. Select the image you stamped in your PDF by clicking on it with the Hand tool (**Figure 8.18**).

   A box appears around the image.

2. Click on one of the corners of the box and drag it to change the size (**Figure 8.19**).

   Hold down the Shift key when you're resizing an image to scale the figure proportionately and from the center.

PASTE CLIPBOARD IMAGE

Using the Snap to Grid Option

The Snap to Grid option is another new feature of Acrobat 7. Use a grid in the background of your PDF to align images, text, graphs, and so on. This feature works very well when you're setting up form fields and helps you make sure all form field boxes are aligned vertically and horizontally, snapping to the grid corners.

You set up Snap to Grid's various options—grid width and height lines, how far the grid is offset from the edge, subdivision (the lines between the grids horizontally and vertically), the grid and guide colors—all from the Preferences dialog box under the Units & Guides pane.

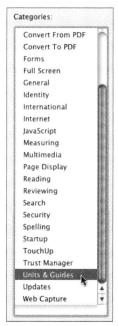

Figure 8.20 Choose Units & Guides from the list that appears on the left of the Preferences dialog.

To set the grid options:

1. Open the Preferences dialog box by pressing Ctrl+K/Command+K.

2. Choose Units & Guides from the list on the left (**Figure 8.20**).

3. Enter the grid size, offset, subdivisions, and color for the grid.

4. Click OK, then choose View > Grid to see the grid you created (**Figure 8.21**).

To activate the Snap to Grid option, choose View > Snap to Grid. This turns on the grid feature. To turn off the Snap to Grid option, choose View > Snap to Grid, or press Ctrl+Shift+U/Command+Shift+U to toggle between turning on and off the Snap to Grid. To see your grid, choose View > Grid or press Control+U/Command+U.

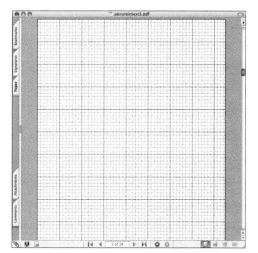

Figure 8.21 Snap to Grid helps you line objects up perfectly.

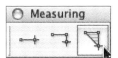

Figure 8.22 Use the Area tool to measure the area of an object.

Figure 8.23 Click on the corners of the object to measure the area.

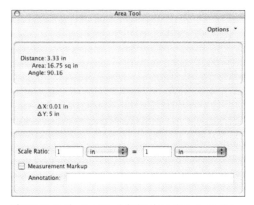

Figure 8.24 The Area Tool dialog box shows you the measurements of your object.

Working with the Measuring Tools

The measuring tools in Acrobat let you measure distances and areas of objects in a PDF document. You can measure the height, width, and area of any object in your PDF. For example, you can measure the sizes of objects in a PDF that was created from a computer-aided design (CAD) drawing.

To measure the area of an object:

1. Open the Measuring toolbar by choosing View > Toolbars > Measuring.

2. Choose the Area tool (**Figure 8.22**).

    This launches the Area tool dialog box. The other tools in the Measuring toolbar are the Distance and the Perimeter tools.

3. Click (but don't drag) on all corners of the object you want to measure (**Figure 8.23**).

    In the Area Tool dialog box, the distance, area, and angle of the object you measured are displayed (**Figure 8.24**). Also shown is the scale ratio of the image. In this image, the scale ratio is 1 inch to 1 inch. You can check the Measurement Markup box and add an annotation to the image you measured. For example, you could add the date the image was taken or the location of the image on your computer. The Options pull-down menu at the top right of the dialog box includes an option that lets you export the measurements into an Excel file.

WORKING WITH THE MEASURING TOOLS

Using Dimensioning Markup

The Dimensioning Markup tool lets you add lines between two points on a PDF document. Use this feature to create measuring lines for objects in your PDF. For example, if you have a blueprint PDF or a house plan PDF, use the Dimensioning markup tool to add the dimension lines and measurements directly on your PDF document.

To add dimension lines to an object:

1. Open the Drawing Markups toolbar by choosing View > Toolbars > Drawing Markups.

2. Choose the Dimensioning tool from the toolbar (**Figure 8.25**).

3. Click and drag along the area where you want to set dimension lines (**Figure 8.26**).

   When you release the mouse button, the dimension line and arrows show up (**Figure 8.27**). There will be a blinking cursor in the middle of the dimensioning lines. This is where you will enter the measurement for the dimension line.

Figure 8.25 Use the Dimensioning tool to create dimension lines.

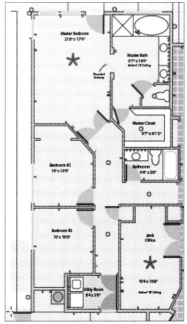

Figure 8.26 To add dimension lines to your PDF, drag with the Dimensioning tool. In this figure, the line is on the left side of the drawing.

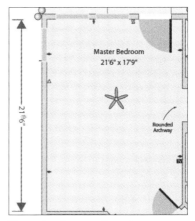

Figure 8.27 Once you have drawn your lines, a line and arrows display the dimension lines you created.

REVIEWING

Adobe has continued to advance the paperless workflow, making life easier for far-flung groups working a single document. In Acrobat, you have several choices for initiating a review of PDF documents. Not only can you send your PDF to colleagues and ask them to export their comments and send them back, you can start an email- or browser-based review that reviewers can access on the Web. And you can make your life easier by using Adobe's Tracker to manage the PDF-reviewing process.

Initiating a Document Review

Sending PDF files to other people for review is a great way to connect people in different locations who work on the same project. You can either email the PDF to someone or post the PDF to a Web page.

To email a PDF document for review:

1. Open the document you want to send for review.

2. In the Tasks toolbar, choose Send for Review > Send by Email for Review. If the Tasks toolbar isn't showing, choose View > Toolbars > Tasks.

   This brings up a Send by Email for Review wizard (**Figure 9.1**). The current open file will appear in the Specify a PDF File to Send by Email for Review box.

3. Leave this file, or choose a different one. Click the Next button.

4. Enter the email address for each individual to whom you want to send the PDF for review (**Figure 9.2**).

   You can customize the reviewing process by clicking the Customize Review Options button to open the Review Options dialog box (**Figure 9.3**). The options you can set in this dialog box are Display Drawing Markup Tools for This Review and Also Allow Users of Free Adobe Reader 7.0 to Participate in This Review. Click OK once you've made your choices. You can set different options for each reviewer by entering his or her address and checking the specific options.

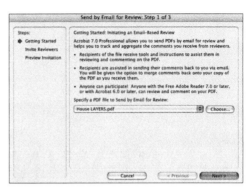

Figure 9.1 Acrobat uses your default email program to send a PDF for review.

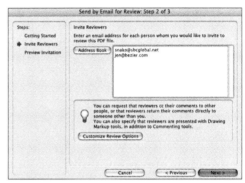

Figure 9.2 Enter recipients' email addresses in the list box.

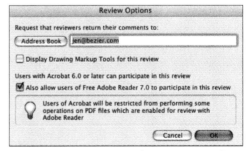

Figure 9.3 You can customize the review process by enabling options in this dialog box.

Figure 9.4 Send the email review.

5. Click the Next button.

The Preview Invitation pane displays the message subject for the email and the message that explains how to perform the reviewing process. You can edit the message or subject as you'd like.

6. Click the Send Invitation button.

The Outgoing Message Notification dialog box launches, letting you know that the PDF has been sent to your default email application (**Figure 9.4**).

Your email program will launch (or come to the front if it is already running). The active PDF file is automatically attached to a new email. Click your Send button, or let the file be sent when your email runs its next schedule.

✔ Tips

- If you find that you want to send a PDF file to additional reviewers who were not on your original list, it's easy to do. Just open the PDF and choose Invite More Reviewers from the Comment and Markup menu in the Tasks toolbar. This launches the Send by Email for Review wizard. Follow the wizard's steps to send the file to more reviewers.

- If you invite Adobe Reader users to participate in the review, this limits the range of comment features that *all* reviewers can use to just those that are available in Reader.

INITIATING A DOCUMENT REVIEW

Web-based document reviews

Acrobat 7 makes it very easy for a corporate workgroup or other large organization to review a document. Reviewers can add comments to a single copy of the document placed at some location on the corporate network or the Internet. This will require some preliminary setup by the company's IT department, but once that is out of the way, any PDF file can be placed on the network for review by specified people.

To set up a PDF file for Web-based review:

1. In the Tasks toolbar, choose Send for Review > Upload for Browser-Based Review (**Figure 9.5**). If the Tasks toolbar isn't showing, choose View > Toolbars > Tasks.

   This launches the Initiate an On-line Review wizard (**Figure 9.6**).

2. The current open file will be listed in the Specify a PDF File to Upload for Browser-Based Review box. Leave this file, or choose a different one. Click the Next button.

3. In the Uploading the PDF step, choose the upload location to put your PDF on a server. Make sure you get the specifics for the server settings from your system administrator.

   Once an appropriate server is available on the network, the Next button will be enabled in the dialog box. Click it.

4. Enter the email address for each person you want to have review the PDF.

5. Click the Send Invitation button.

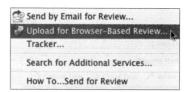

Figure 9.5 You can upload a PDF to a server for a Web-based review.

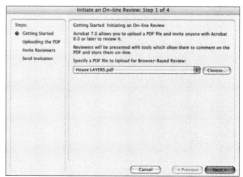

Figure 9.6 Use the Initiate an On-line Review wizard to take you through the process step by step.

To send your reviewers a reminder:

1. With the PDF as your active document, choose Comments > Send Review Reminder.

   This will open your email program with a Reminder note in the subject line (**Figure 9.7**) and the reviewers' names in the To: area.

2. Delete or add additional names.

3. Click the Send button.

   The reminder email is sent to specific reviewers.

Figure 9.7 Remind your reviewers by email.

Participating in a PDF Review

When you've been invited to review a PDF document by email, just opening the attachment begins the review process. Working in the Web browser window, you can add your comments to the PDF file and upload them for other reviewers to see, or save the file to your computer for offline reviewing. You can download other reviewers' comments as well.

To review a PDF in a Web browser:

1. Once you receive an email inviting you to participate in a review, open the attached file.

   This will launch your Web browser, displaying the PDF file that resides on the remote server. In addition, you'll notice that your browser window now includes a set of Acrobat toolbars that you can use to comment on the document.

2. Using the tools in the Commenting toolbar, add your comments to the PDF file online in the Web browser. (See Chapters 7 and 8 for information on working with these tools.)

   You can also save a copy on your computer so that you can work offline.

To send comments:

1. When you've entered your comments into the PDF file and you're ready to send, choose Comments > Send Comments (**Figure 9.8**).

   This opens the Send Comments dialog box (**Figure 9.9**).

Figure 9.8 You can send comments by email.

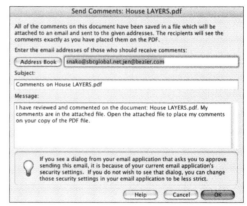

Figure 9.9 The Send Comments dialog box launches where you can enter the email addresses of your recipients.

Figure 9.10 You can reply to any comment.

Figure 9.11 Enter your reply to the note or comment.

2. Click OK to send the commented file.

If you're in an email-based review, the Outgoing Message Notification dialog box opens, letting you know the PDF has been sent to your default email application. Your email program will launch or become active. The active PDF file is automatically attached to a new email. Click your Send button, or let the file be sent when your email runs its next schedule.

If you are conducting a Web-based review, your comments are uploaded to the server without your email software being involved.

To comment on another reviewer's comment:

1. With the Hand tool, open the note and choose Reply from the Options arrow menu.

   or

   Right-click/Control-click the note and choose Reply from the contextual toolbar that appears (**Figure 9.10**).

   This opens a new note box in both the Document pane and the Comments List; the box has the heading "Reply" (**Figure 9.11**).

2. Enter your reply or replies to the note.

   If you notice that in the Reply box there's more than one reply, you can view them one at a time by clicking the Next Comment arrow, or you can click the View All button on the toolbar to see all replies.

PARTICIPATING IN A PDF REVIEW

Viewing Comments

You can view comments on the page or at the bottom of the screen, or hide them entirely. Simply choose View > Show Comments List, or choose Show Comments List from the Comments menu. When the Comments list is visible at the bottom of your document window (**Figure 9.12**), you can hide it again by choosing View > Hide Comments List.

These are the other viewing options in the Commenting toolbar's Show menu (**Figure 9.13**):

- **Commenting Toolbar** shows/hides the Commenting toolbar.

- **Drawing Markup Toolbar** shows/hides the Drawing Markups toolbar.

- **Show/Hide Comments List** displays or hides the Comments list at the bottom of the screen.

- **Show/Hide All Comments** shows or hides all comments added to the PDF file.

- **Show by Type** lets you choose whether to view all comments or a single type of comment (**Figure 9.14**), such as highlights or text insertions.

- **Show by Reviewer** lets you filter comments according to who wrote them.

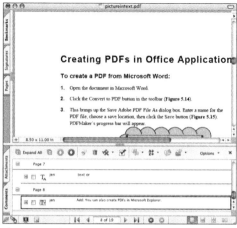

Figure 9.12 The comments are viewable at the bottom of your document window.

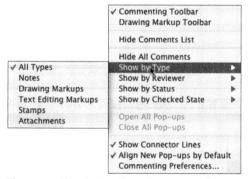

Figure 9.13 Select the Commenting toolbar to access a variety of viewing options.

Figure 9.14 Show by Type lists all comments of specific types.

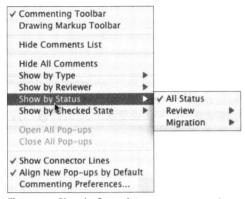

Figure 9.15 Show by Status lets you see comments that have been accepted, rejected, and so forth.

◆ **Show by Status** lets you see comments that have been accepted, rejected, cancelled, or completed or that have no status (**Figure 9.15**).

◆ **Show by Checked State** lists comments according to whether they've been checked.

In the Comments pane on the left side of the main Acrobat window, there are more items and commands for working with your comments (**Figure 9.16**):

◆ **Expand All Elements in the Panel** lets you expand and view all comments in the Comments pane and information such as author, type of comment, and date.

◆ **Collapse All Elements in the Panel** collapses the comments to show just the page on which a comment resides.

◆ **Go to the Next Comment** takes you to the next consecutive comment.

◆ **Go to the Previous Comment** returns you to the previous comment.

(continues on next page)

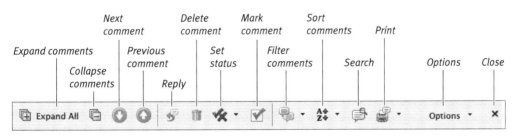

Figure 9.16 The buttons along the top of the Comments pane give you still more options.

VIEWING COMMENTS

◆ **Reply to the Selected Comment**
allows you to reply to someone's comment. You first choose the comment and then click the Reply button. A new line will appear in the Comments list for you to enter your reply (**Figure 9.17**).

◆ **Delete the Selected Comment**
removes the comment you selected.

◆ **Set the Comment Status** shows whether the comment was accepted, rejected, cancelled, or completed. Select the comment first, and then choose one of the status options. The status option shows up in a line below the comment.

◆ **Checkmark** marks the selected comment, which is useful for keeping track of which comments you've looked at.

◆ **Filter** lets you filter the various comment types as explained earlier.

◆ **Sort By** lets you change the order in which comments are listed (by type, page, author, date, color, checkmark status, or status by person).

◆ **Search** lets you search the comments for a specific word or phrase.

◆ **Print Comments** allows you to print a summary of comments, create a PDF, and several more options, which are covered in the section "Summarizing Comments," later in this chapter.

◆ **Options** features a menu of commands, such as Summarize Comments, Import Comments, Export Selected Comments, Tracker (for Reviews), and Scan for Comments. For more on summarizing, see the tasks later in this chapter.

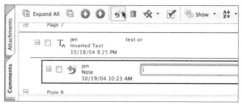

Figure 9.17 You can type in a reply in response to another person's comment.

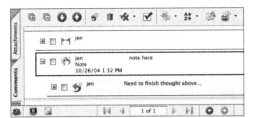

Figure 9.18 Select a comment by clicking it.

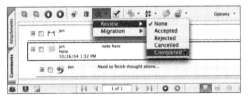

Figure 9.19 Choose a status for your comment.

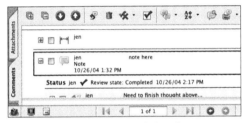

Figure 9.20 The status appears below the comment.

Changing the Status of a Comment

As you read over reviewed documents, you can make it clear which comments you've read by changing their status to Accepted, Rejected, Cancelled, or Completed. This is particularly helpful when you want to show or hide certain comments. For example, after changing the status of several comments, you can sort by status to show only Accepted ones.

To change the status of a comment:

1. In the document that has been reviewed, choose Comments > Show Comments List or click on the Comments tab.

    The Comments pane opens below your document.

2. Select the comment you want to change by clicking it in the Comments list (**Figure 9.18**).

3. Choose an option from the Set Status menu in the Comments pane toolbar (**Figure 9.19**). Choose from the Review or Migration pop-up submenus. (You'll learn about the Migration options in an upcoming section.)

    The comment's status is shown below the comment (**Figure 9.20**).

✔ Tip

- You can also set status by right-clicking/ Control-clicking the comment in the Document pane and choosing a status from the Set Status menu item in the pop-up menu that appears.

Summarizing Comments

Acrobat provides a method for summarizing all the comments in a document quickly. This feature actually creates a new PDF file with the comments listed and labeled, including their type, author, and date. You can view the comments in the bottom half of the document window. The Comments List toolbar lets you access the commenting menu items quickly.

Figure 9.21 You can summarize the comments from your reviewed document.

To create a summary of the comments in a document:

1. Choose Summarize Comments from the Options menu in the Comments list (**Figure 9.21**).

   or

   Choose Summarize Comments from the Comment & Markup menu in the Tasks toolbar.

   The Summarize Options dialog box appears.

2. Choose a layout; specify how you want to sort comments—by author, date, page, or type of annotation; indicate which comments you want to include; and choose a font size (**Figure 9.22**).

   Under the Choose a Layout option, you can specify how the summary document shows comments, such as with or without connector lines (lines drawn from the note to the area of reference in the PDF text). As you select each radio button, the icon in the dialog box changes to show a representation of that choice. Other options include summarizing all comments or only currently shown comments, as well as choosing a font size for the summary.

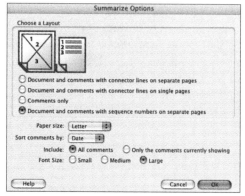

Figure 9.22 Select a layout, sorting option, and other settings for summarizing your comments.

Acrobat will churn a bit if you have a large number of comments. Then a new document appears, with all comments listed (**Figure 9.23**).

After you've viewed the comments, you can save the PDF file, print it, or close it without saving it.

✔ Tips

■ I suggest that you select Document and Comments with Connector Lines on Single Pages so that you can see what the comments refer to. This may result in a larger file, but it's easier to understand.

■ Text that has been marked up with the Highlight tools, Drawing tools, and Pencil tools also appears in the summary, along with notes of any attached documents or sound files.

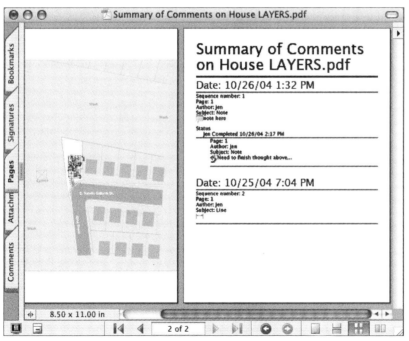

Figure 9.23 A new document lists the comments as a separate file.

SUMMARIZING COMMENTS

Deleting Comments

To clean up a document, you may want to delete some of the comments that have been added by reviewers—for example, any comments that were rejected or cancelled.

To delete a comment:

1. Select a comment in the Document pane and press the Backspace/Delete key.

2. If you have the Comments pane open, you can select the comment and click the trashcan icon in the Comments pane toolbar (**Figure 9.24**).

   or

   Press the Backspace /Delete key.

✔ Tip

■ You can get the comment back if you Undo (Ctrl-Z/Command-Z) right after you delete it.

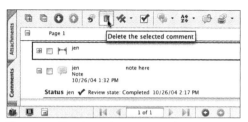

Figure 9.24 Use the trashcan or press the Backspace/Delete key to remove a comment.

Figure 9.25 Choose a format for exporting your comments.

Exporting and Importing Comments

Whether or not you're directly participating in a review, you can import others' comments into your PDF file and export your own comments from Acrobat and save them as a Form Data Format (FDF) file, which contains only the comments and not the whole file. Although it's possible to open an FDF file with a text editor, it won't be very useful; the best way to apply comments to the document is to have the original or a copy of the PDF file that is being commented on. Import the comments to that original PDF, and the comments will line up in the correct locations. This is especially useful when dealing with a large PDF document with many pages. Exporting the comments will only retain the comments and their locations so that when you import the user's comments, the comments will show up in the Comments pane and in the right locations in the PDF file.

To export comments:

1. In the PDF file with your comments, choose Comments > Export Comments.

   You can do this as a reviewer, as an offline reviewer, or as the initiator of the review so that everyone can see your comments.

2. In the Export Comments dialog box that appears, choose Acrobat FDF Files or Acrobat XFDF Files from the Format menu (**Figure 9.25**).

continues on next page

3. Choose a save location for the exported file on your computer, and enter a name for the file.

4. Click Save.

This will create the FDF file with only the comments and save it on your computer. You can email your comments to other reviewers, and they'll appear in the same place in the original PDF when they're imported.

To export selected comments:

1. In the Comments pane, select the comments to be exported (**Figure 9.26**). Select a single comment by clicking it; select multiple comments by Ctrl/Command-clicking.

2. Choose Export Selected Comments from the Options menu in the Comments list (**Figure 9.27**).

The Export Comments dialog box appears.

3. Choose Acrobat FDF Files or Acrobat XFDF Files from the Format menu.

4. Choose a save location for the exported comments and enter a filename.

5. Click Save.

You'll have a document that contains your comments, which you can send to another reviewer. The recipient can then import your comments into the original PDF file.

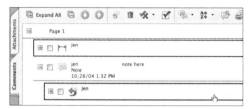

Figure 9.26 You can select specific comments to export.

Figure 9.27 Select this command to export selected comments.

Figure 9.28 Choose Comments > Import Comments to import comments into your PDF document.

To import comments:

1. Open the document into which you want to import comments.

2. Choose Comments > Import Comments (**Figure 9.28**).

   This opens the Import Comments dialog box, which you can use to navigate to the FDF file on your computer. (You probably received the FDF file by email from another reviewer.)

3. Once you locate the FDF file that you want to import, click Select or double-click the name of the file (**Figure 9.29**).

   You'll get a message saying the import was successful (**Figure 9.30**), and the comments will appear in the proper areas in the document and in the Comments list.

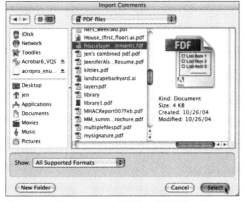

Figure 9.29 You can import FDF or XFDF files into your PDF document.

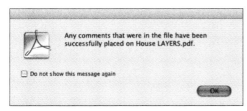

Figure 9.30 A message will appear letting you know the import was successful.

Export Comments from Acrobat into Word (Windows)

New to Acrobat is the ability to export the comments from a PDF file directly into Microsoft Word (Windows only). The exported comments will show up as a text bubble in Word 2002 or later. You can also choose whether to delete any text that a reviewer has asked (in a comment) to have crossed out or inserted into the Word document. Comments can also be imported into the engineering program AutoCad (from Autodesk) just as you can in Word.

To export a comment into Word (Windows):

1. Choose Comments > Export Comments > To Word (**Figure 9.31**).
   This launches the Import Comments from Adobe Acrobat dialog box, which describes the process for importing the comments into Word (**Figure 9.32**).

2. Click OK to begin the import process. In the next dialog box, choose the file you want to take the comments from; then choose the Word file into which you want to put the comments.

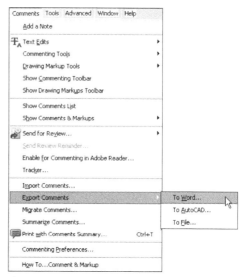

Figure 9.31 You can export comments from Acrobat into Word.

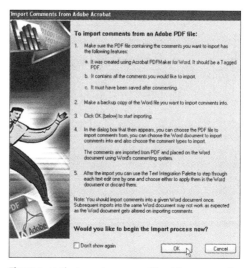

Figure 9.32 The import process will put the comments into the chosen Word file.

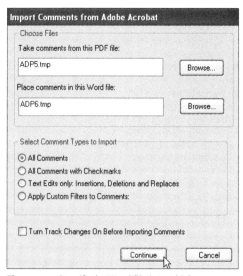

Figure 9.33 Specify the Word file into which you want to export the comments.

3. Click the Continue button to continue this importing process. Enter the name of the Word document into which you want to import the comments (**Figure 9.33**).

4. Open the Word file to see the comments shown as text bubbles in the document.

✔ Tips

■ It is important to back up the Word document before attempting to insert the Acrobat comments into it. Acrobat will modify the Word document and, if something goes wrong, could conceivably corrupt it.

■ The wording in the dialog boxes can be confusing. Although you select Export to Word, the dialog boxes all make reference to "Importing" comments. Just keep in mind that from the point of view of Word, the comments are being imported.

EXPORT COMMENTS FROM ACROBAT INTO WORD

Managing a Review with Tracker

Acrobat's Tracker keeps track of all the PDF documents you've sent or received for email- and browser-based reviews. Use it to send a reminder, invite more reviewers, remove reviewed files, and open the PDF file on which a review is based. The Manage option also lets you email all reviewers, send a reminder, and go back online when you've been reviewing offline.

To work with Tracker:

1. Choose Comments > Tracker.

   or

   Choose Comment & Markup > Tracker from the Tasks toolbar.

   or

   Choose View > Tracker (**Figure 9.34**). This opens the Tracker dialog box (**Figure 9.35**).

2. Choose the review you want to alter.

3. In the Tracker dialog box you can choose to open the PDF (**Figure 9.36**), remove the PDF, or select one of the options from the Manage pop-up menu, such as Email All Reviewers, Send Review Reminder, or Invite Additional Reviewers.

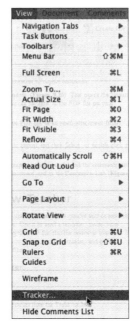

Figure 9.34 Choose View > Tracker to start the process of keeping track of your PDF commented documents.

Figure 9.35 The Tracker dialog box lists all of your reviewed PDFs.

Figure 9.36 You can open or delete your PDF in the Tracker dialog box, or choose a Manage option.

MANAGING A REVIEW WITH TRACKER

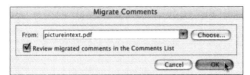

Figure 9.37 Choose Comments > Migrate Comments to add comments to a revised file.

Migrating Comments

Once you have imported comments into a PDF file and revised that document, more comments may come along that need to be imported. To import additional comments into a revised PDF file, use the Migrate Comments feature. Migrate Comments will put the additional comments in the correct areas of the PDF document that you are reviewing.

To migrate comments into a PDF file:

1. Choose Comments > Migrate Comments. This launches the Migrate Comments dialog box.

2. Pick a commented file in the From pop-up menu or click Choose to pick a file—the original, unrevised PDF file. Then click OK (**Figure 9.37**).

   The new comments are added to the file.

Migratory Habits

Acrobat 7's Migrate Comments feature is actually rather impressive. The idea is that you have revised your document based on comments you've received; you regenerated the PDF file from your layout document. At a later time, some additional comments based on the original, unrevised document come in (there's always someone who's late). You can import comments from the original PDF file into your new PDF file and Acrobat will do its best to place the comments in the correct position in the new file. For example, a "highlighted text" comment will still highlight the same text in the revised document, even though that text is now in a different position on the page (or even on a different page).

MIGRATING COMMENTS

Printing a Comments Summary

You can create a comments summary file to view as a PDF within Acrobat. Take that a step further and you can print out the document with the comments summary. You would do this, for example, if you wanted to fax the comments to someone who's not on the reviewing team, or to have a hard copy of the comments on the reviewed PDF file.

To print a document with comments:

1. Choose File > Print with Comments Summary (**Figure 9.38**).

   or

   Choose Comments > Print with Comments Summary.

   This launches the Summarize Options dialog box.

2. Choose a layout, paper size, the method for sorting comments, which comments to include, and font size. Then click OK (**Figure 9.39**).

   The Print dialog box is launched.

3. Enter the number of copies, pages to be printed, and so on, and then click the Print button.

   The PDF document is printed with the comments summary.

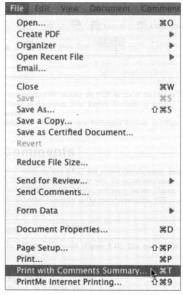

Figure 9.38 You can print the comments summary.

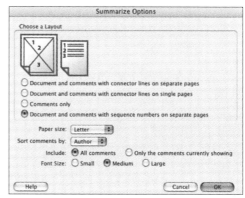

Figure 9.39 Choose which comments you want to see and how you want them to be presented.

10

FORMS

Interactivity. That's what electronic publishing is all about. The 1980s vision of a paperless society is still pretty far off for several reasons. One of those reasons in the past has been that electronic media have had no really good means of collecting feedback. Users have not been able to input information in a way that imitates using a pen or pencil to fill out paper forms. That situation is changing, and Acrobat's forms capabilities are evidence.

Forms allow people who view a document with Acrobat, or Adobe Reader, to fill in text fields, choose options, click buttons, and even send information over the Internet automatically.

For those who want to create PDF forms, Acrobat lets you keep the layout, fonts, and information in the form constant across different platforms. Setting up forms is designed to be as simple as possible, with a straightforward list of options and a Form tool to assist you.

Creating Form Documents and Fields

A *form document* is simply a PDF file that is designed to gather information—such as name, address, and cost and quantity of an item. The PDF has a set of *form fields,* graphical items such as a check box or text field, which is where users enter such information. You can use any program that lets you print to PDF to design the look of a form and then save the design as a PDF. For instance, you could create an invoice in Microsoft Excel, print it to a PDF, and then open it in Acrobat to turn it into a form document (**Figure 10.1**). On the Windows platform, you can also use Adobe Designer to create and design a variety of forms. (See the last section in this chapter, "Using Designer to Create Your Form.")

Once you have saved your PDF file from within another application (such as Excel or Corel's CorelDraw), you can open it in Acrobat and add form fields to it. Users can modify form fields; for instance, they can click a check box or type in a text box, as long as they have Acrobat 4.0 or Reader 4.0 or later. Acrobat can create the following types of fields:

◆ **Buttons** trigger an action, such as opening a file or playing a sound.

◆ **Check boxes** let you respond to a yes-or-no question by checking a box.

◆ **Combo boxes** offer a pop-up menu of items to choose from.

◆ **List boxes** display a list of items that the reader can scroll through to choose one or multiple items.

◆ **Radio buttons** let you choose one item from a list of mutually exclusive items.

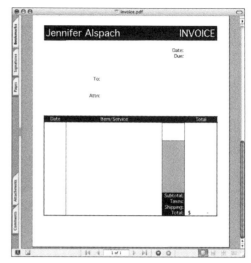

Figure 10.1 We created an invoice using Microsoft Excel, then brought it into Acrobat to add the form fields.

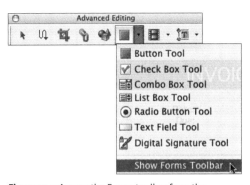

Figure 10.2 Access the Forms toolbar from the Advanced Editing toolbar.

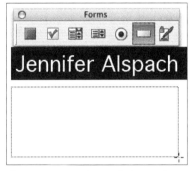

Figure 10.3 Drag a box to designate the size of your field.

◆ **Text fields** collect textual information such as name and address.

◆ **Digital signatures** create a field for you to digitally sign a document (see Chapter 14 for more about digital signatures).

In addition, you can control various elements of these fields, such as their appearance and behavior.

You create form fields primarily within Acrobat, although other Adobe applications (such as Designer, InDesign, FrameMaker, and Illustrator) allow you to specify form fields and buttons that should appear in the document when it is turned into a PDF file.

To create a form field in Acrobat:

1. Choose View > Toolbars > Advanced Editing. From the Advanced Editing toolbar, choose Show Forms Toolbar from the Button menu (**Figure 10.2**).

   or

   Choose Tools > Advanced Editing > Show Forms Toolbar.

2. Choose a type of form field to create, then drag a marquee across the area you'd like to designate as a form field (**Figure 10.3**).

   For this example, I chose to create a text field to add an address.

   When you release the mouse button, the Text Field Properties dialog box appears.

(continues on next page)

CREATING FORM DOCUMENTS AND FIELDS

3. On the General tab, enter a name for the text field and some text for the tool tip (tool tip text will appear as a help note when the user rests the mouse pointer over a button, note, or form field) (**Figure 10.4**).

Acrobat provides a default internal name for your form field; you may type in your own name (it can be any arbitrary text), though there's little reason to do this with simple forms. Also, keep in mind that this name is for internal use by JavaScripts and Acrobat itself; it will not be visible to the user.

For this example, I entered "Name" in the name field and "Please enter your full name here" for the tool tip.

You can also specify options in the Common Properties area, such as the form field visibility and orientation (0, 90, 180, or 270 degrees).

4. On the Appearance tab, specify how you want the form field to look. Choose a border color, fill color, line thickness, and line style. Also select a font, font size, and text color (**Figure 10.5**).

5. On the Options tab, choose an alignment from the pop-up menu.

You can choose from a few other options, such as Check Spelling and Scroll Long Lines of Text (which will add scroll bars to a form field if the user enters text that exceeds the boundaries of the field).

You can also add an *action*—an activity that Acrobat will perform when the user interacts with the form field. For instance, you can add an action that tells Acrobat to open another file or go to a Web page when the user clicks a button. I won't add an action for this example. (For more information on actions, see "Setting Properties" later in this chapter.)

The Format, Validate, and Calculate tabs are used for form fields with numeric values, which we'll discuss later in this chapter.

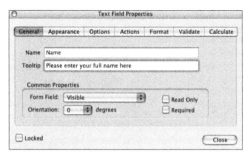

Figure 10.4 The Text Field Properties dialog box appears.

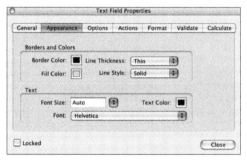

Figure 10.5 Choose how you want the field to look.

Figure 10.6 The Fields palette is under the Navigation submenu of the View menu.

6. Click Close.

After you create form fields, you can view and access them quickly in the Fields palette.

✔ Tips

■ The default text field settings give you a one-line text field that is flush left, contains no "dummy" text, and has no border or background color.

■ After the fields are created, you can move from field to field in the order they were created by using the Tab key. Pressing Shift+Tab will take you to the preceding field.

■ To edit any form field, double-click the box surrounding the form field with the Select Object tool (the one that looks like a standard black arrow in the Advanced Editing toolbar). This action opens the Field Properties dialog box, where you can make changes. Field properties are covered later in this chapter.

To view fields in the Fields palette:

1. Choose View > Navigation > Fields.

The Fields palette appears as a floating palette (**Figure 10.6**). All existing fields are listed in the palette.

2. Double-click a field icon in the list to make it the active field in the document.

Setting Properties

Use the Properties dialog box to determine how each field looks and behaves. The dialog box contains a variety of options that change for each field type. You can set the font and text style of text boxes, designate various actions that will occur when a user interacts with the form in certain ways, and write scripts that calculate or validate form data. This section discusses setting the properties of a text box, which offers the widest range of options:

◆ The **General** pane has settings for the name, tool tip text, and common properties such as form field visibility, orientation, and whether a form field is read-only (not editable by users) or required (users have to fill it in before closing the form). The General properties, as well as the properties for Appearance and Actions, are identical for all form field types.

◆ The **Appearance** pane offers settings for the border color, fill color, line thickness, line style, font, font size, and text color of the field box.

◆ The **Options** pane provides settings for the alignment of text within a box, and lets you specify whether you want to automatically scroll long text to fit within a text box, among other options. . The options on this pane vary according to the type of form field you're working with.

◆ The **Actions** pane enables you to set triggers and actions linked to a particular field. Choose an action and trigger, such as clicking with the mouse button over a defined area (trigger) to make a sound play (action). Other types of triggers include releasing the mouse button over a form field or simply rolling the mouse pointer over a field. The range of actions Acrobat can carry out in response to these events is very broad, including such things as going to another page (as a link does), playing a movie, executing a JavaScript, or executing a menu item.

◆ The **Format** pane lets you specify the format for items that are represented by numbers, such as percentages, date, and time. For instance, you can choose how many decimal points to display for numbers and whether dates will include just the month and day (12/8) or the month, day, and year (12/8/04). If you don't see the item you're looking for, check the Special category. You can even create your own item under Custom, which is an advanced task (you'll probably need to find documentation on this topic before trying it).

You can access the Format pane only when you're working with text and combo text fields.

◆ The **Validate** pane enables you to set a field to be validated. For instance, Acrobat can check to see if the text a user enters in a serial number field looks like a valid serial number. You can access the Validate pane only when you're working with text and combo text fields.

◆ The **Calculate** pane lets you specify that the value of a text field is the result of a calculation. That calculation may be the sum, difference, or product (or other type of result) of two or more other form fields. For example, the field could contain the product of quantity multiplied by price per item. You may also specify a more complex calculation using Simplified Field Notation or JavaScript.

As with Format and Validate, you can access the Calculate pane only when you're working with text and combo text fields.

SETTING PROPERTIES

To set the appearance of text fields:

1. With the Text Field or Select Object tool, double-click the field for which you want to set properties.

   The Text Field Properties dialog box appears.

2. Click the Appearance tab.

   The Appearance options are displayed (**Figure 10.7**).

3. If you'd like the field to have a border, click the Border Color check box and then choose the color by clicking the box to the right of the check box.

   You can also set a fill color for within the border.

   The Color Picker native to your computer system appears, allowing you to choose from among a wide variety of colors.

4. If you've chosen to place a border on the field, you can change the width and style by making choices from the Line Thickness and Line Style pop-up menus.

5. In the Text section, choose the font you want for user-entered text from the Font pop-up menu.

   You can also modify the color and size of the text. All of the changes you make are immediately visible on the field box you have chosen.

6. Click the Close button to close the Properties dialog box.

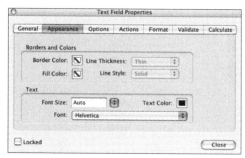

Figure 10.7 Set how you want the field to look in the Appearance tab.

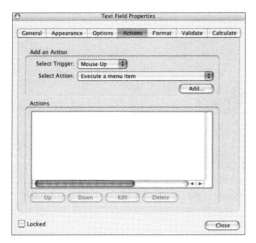

Figure 10.8 Click the Actions tab to set an action.

Figure 10.9 Select an action from the pop-up menu.

Adding Actions to Fields

You can also add actions to a field. As explained earlier in this section, an action is some activity that Acrobat carries out when the user clicks or otherwise interacts with a form field. Each action has two parts to it:

◆ A *trigger,* which is something the user does that initiates the action (for example, releasing the mouse button when the pointer is within the field's boundary)

◆ An *action,* which is what Acrobat does in response to the trigger: play a movie, move to a different page within the document, execute a JavaScript. Acrobat has a large number of actions you can associate with a form field.

As an example, let's attach a *submit* action to an Acrobat button field. Assume that we've created and distributed a form and we need to get the data from the user's form when the user fills it out. We can use the submit action to have the document's form data sent to a URL or email address. In this example, we'll have Acrobat email the form data to us so we can enter it into a database.

To add an action to a form field:

1. Double-click the button field to which you want to add an action.

   The button's Properties dialog box appears.

2. Choose the Actions tab to see your choices (**Figure 10.8**).

3. Choose a trigger from the Select Trigger pop-up list; then select an action from the Select Action pop-up list (**Figure 10.9**).

   For this example, choose Submit a Form as the action. For the trigger, choose Mouse Up so that the form will be sent when the user clicks and then releases the mouse button over the button field we're creating.

(continues on next page)

4. Click the Add button.

This adds the action to the form field and presents you with a dialog box that collects information needed for the particular action. In our case, Acrobat needs to know where to send the form data.

5. Enter the data requested by the dialog box (**Figure 10.10**).

In our case, we need to supply the following:

▲ The URL to which we want to send our form data. To email the data, use an address in this form: mailto:receivedata@mycompany.com.

The *mailto:* tells Acrobat that this is an email address. The form data will be sent to this address as an attachment. The URL could also have been the HTTP address of a server that's prepared to receive the data (this needs to be set up by an IT person).

▲ The format in which the data should be sent. FDF (Form Data Format) is the most common. The email attachment will consist of a file containing only the form data. This file may be imported into a copy of the original form to see the original form entries.

▲ Which fields should have their data sent. All Fields is usually the best choice.

▲ Whether dates should be converted to a standard format. This is necessary only if you are submitting the form data to a server program that needs to be able to process the data automatically.

6. Click Close to set the action.

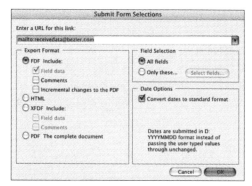

Figure 10.10 Enter the URL or email address that will receive the form data.

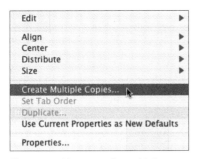

Figure 10.11 You can make multiple copies of a field you've created.

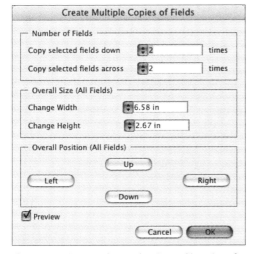

Figure 10.12 You can change the size and location of all of the fields at one time.

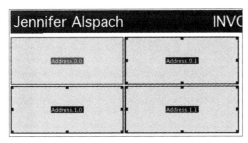

Figure 10.13 Click OK to see your multiple fields.

Adding Fields

Once you understand how to create fields, you'll probably want to add more. A quick way to add form fields is in a column spreadsheet form. Once you have a certain look and size for a form field, use the Create Multiple Copies feature to make more fields that are evenly distributed and spaced apart nicely. After creating the copies, you can then edit the individual boxes as you like.

To create a table of form fields:

1. Choose the Select Object tool from the Advanced Editing toolbar.

2. Right-click/Control-click the field you want to copy and choose Create Multiple Copies from the contextual menu (**Figure 10.11**).

   This launches the Create Multiple Copies of Fields dialog box.

3. Enter the number of fields you want to copy down and across (**Figure 10.12**).

   This will affect all fields that you are duplicating. You can also choose the Overall position: you can move all of the fields up, down, left, or right. Just click the appropriate button to move the fields. Keep in mind that you can always drag the field to a new position using the form field tool that created the original field.

4. Click OK to view the group of new fields on your document (**Figure 10.13**).

191

To adjust a field's position and size:

1. From the Forms toolbar, choose the tool you used to create the particular field that you want to adjust.

   or

   Use the Select Object tool from the Advanced Editing toolbar to select any type of form field, no matter which tool you used to create the field.

2. Click the field you want to modify. Handles and a red line appear around the field (**Figure 10.14**).

3. Click the center of the field and drag it to move the field.

4. Drag the corner handles of the field to resize it (**Figure 10.15**).

5. When you've finished, make sure that the field is the correct size by choosing the Hand tool and entering sample information (**Figure 10.16**).

✔ Tips

- You can be more precise in your adjustments if you zoom in before you drag. Press and hold Ctrl+spacebar/Command+ spacebar to access the Zoom In tool quickly.

- Use the arrow keys to nudge the position of a selected form field in the appropriate direction. If you hold down the Shift key and use the arrow keys, it will change the size of the field a pixel at a time.

Figure 10.14 Use the handles to change the size of your field.

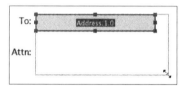

Figure 10.15 Drag the corner handles to resize horizontally and vertically at the same time.

Figure 10.16 Enter sample information to check your field size.

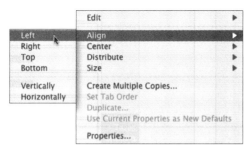

Figure 10.17 Choose Align from the contextual menu.

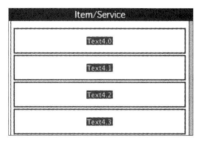

Figure 10.18 When you choose Align the fields will line up.

To align form fields:

1. With the Text Field tool active, click the field with which you want to align other fields.

2. While holding down the Shift key, select the other form fields you want to align.

3. Right-click/Control-click on the form field that you want the others to align to and choose Align and an alignment option from the contextual menu (**Figure 10.17**).

   The final result shows the aligned text fields (**Figure 10.18**). The field you right-clicked/Control-clicked will be highlighted in red rather than blue; this field will remain fixed in position while all of the other fields are moved to align with it.

ADDING FIELDS

Creating Combo Box Fields

Combo boxes are pop-up menus with editable text boxes attached to them. The pop-up menu allows the PDF author to define the most common or desired choices for the text box, but you can make the field editable to allow the user to enter a choice that you as the author didn't provide.

To define a combo box field:

1. Choose the Combo Box tool from the Forms toolbar.

2. Drag to draw the field on the page (**Figure 10.19**), or click to select an existing field.

3. When the Combo Box Properties dialog box appears, choose the General tab and name the field, and (if you like) type a brief description in the Tooltip text box. Choose any desired settings from the Common Properties area.

4. Click the Appearance tab, and enter the border color, fill color, line thickness, line style, font, font size, and text color.

5. Choose the Options tab. In the Item text box, enter an item you want to have included in the combo box, then click the Add button to have it listed (**Figure 10.20**).

   You could use the combo box to show specific items, such as a list of items you want to sell, or use it to give users options for displaying the date (such as mm/dd/yyyy or m/d/y).

Figure 10.19 Create a new field or select an existing one.

Figure 10.20 Click the Add button to add a new item.

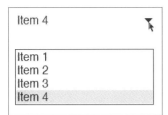

Figure 10.21 Use the Hand tool to choose an item from the combo box pop-up menu.

6. Enter an export value if you want, and check any of the other options on the Options tab (choose from Sort Items, Allow User to Enter Custom Text, Check Spelling, or Commit Selected Value Immediately).

An *export value* is the internal value associated with an item in the menu. As far as Acrobat is concerned, this is the menu item. If you don't supply an export value, then Acrobat will use the *item text*, the text you entered in step 5, as the export value.

7. Click the Close button when you've finished.

When you switch to the Hand tool, you'll be able to choose an item from the combo box field's pop-up menu (**Figure 10.21**).

✔ Tips

■ To change the order of items you've added to a Combo box, select an item in the Item List box, then click the Up or Down button to move the added items to different positions.

■ Click the Sort Items check box to list the items in alphabetical order, regardless of the order in which they were entered.

■ To remove an item from the list, select it and then click the Delete button.

Creating Check Box Fields

Check boxes can work individually or in sets. Within a set of check boxes, one, none, all, or any combination of the boxes can be checked (activated). Check boxes are flexible and independent. Clicking any check box usually has no effect on any other check box within that set.

To create a check box field:

1. Choose the Check Box tool from the Forms toolbar (**Figure 10.22**).

2. Drag to draw the field on the page.
   The Check Box Properties dialog box appears.
   In the Check Box Properties dialog box, there are only four tabs to choose from: General, Appearance, Options, and Actions.

3. Choose the General tab and name the field, and (if you like) type a brief description in the Tooltip text box. Choose settings in the Common Properties area, as you did in previous tasks.

4. Specify settings in the General, Appearance, and Actions panes as in previous tasks.

5. On the Options tab, choose a style for your check box from the pop-up menu (**Figure 10.23**).

6. Enter a value in the Export Value text box.
   This text will be the text box's value if you check it. "Yes" is the default setting.

7. If you'd like the field to be selected by default, click the Check Box Is Checked by Default check box.

8. Click Close.

9. Change to the Hand tool to display the check box (**Figure 10.24**).

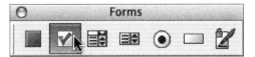

Figure 10.22 You'll find the Check Box tool on the Forms toolbar.

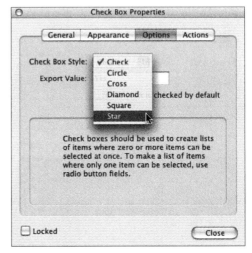

Figure 10.23 Choose a check box style on the Options tab of the Check Box Properties dialog box.

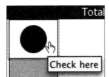

Figure 10.24 Use the Hand tool to view your check box.

Figure 10.25 Drag out the size you want the digital signature field to be.

Creating Digital Signature Fields

You can add a field for users to include a *digital signature,* which can be a handwritten name, a logo or other graphic symbol, or text. Set up the field as you want it to appear on your form. When users receive the file, they can add a signature after filling out the form. For instance, you might use a digital signature field to let users authorize a purchase. (To find out how to create a digital signature, see Chapter 14.)

To create a digital signature field:

1. In the Advanced Editing toolbar, click on the arrow next to the Button tool and choose the Digital Signature Field tool.

   or

   Choose the Digital Signature tool from the Forms toolbar.

   If the Forms toolbar isn't on screen, choose Tools > Advanced Editing > Show Forms Toolbar.

2. Drag to draw a field on the page (**Figure 10.25**).

3. When the Digital Signature Properties dialog box appears, choose the General tab to name the field, and (if you like) type a brief description in the Tooltip text box.

   (continues on next page)

CREATING DIGITAL SIGNATURE FIELDS

4. Click the Appearance tab to change the border color, background color, line thickness, and line style of the field.

You can also change the font, font size, and text color (in this case, the color of the text that shows in the field).

5. Select the Signed tab. This tab lets you specify what happens after the form is signed. Choose from Nothing Happens when Signed, Mark as Read-Only (choose the fields from a pop-up menu), or This Script Executes when Field is Signed. Click the Close button when you've finished (**Figure 10.26**).

When the people who receive your form use the signature field, Acrobat will ask them to sign the document. It will also ask for a password.

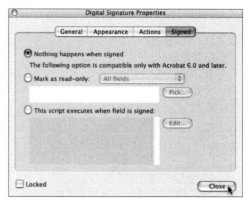

Figure 10.26 Click the Close button to set the field.

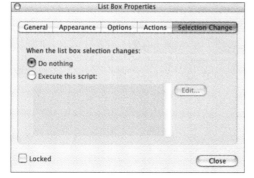

Figure 10.27 Choose the List Box tool from the Forms toolbar.

Figure 10.28 The Selection Change tab lets you specify what will happen when the user selects an item in the list box.

Creating List Box Fields

A list box displays a drop-down list of items for the user to choose from. The user can pick one or multiple items. If there are more items in the list than can fit in the box, scroll bars let the user scroll through all the items in the list.

To create a list box field:

1. Choose the List Box tool from the Forms toolbar (**Figure 10.27**).

2. Drag to draw the field on the page.

   The List Box Properties dialog box appears.

   The List Box Properties dialog box features five tabs: General, Appearance, Options, Actions, and Selection Change.

3. Choose the General tab and name the field, and (if you like) type a brief description in the Tooltip text box. Choose settings from the Common Properties area as you did in previous tasks.

4. Set items in the General, Appearance, Options, and Actions panes as in previous tasks.

5. On the Selection Change tab, specify what you want to have happen when the list box selection changes (**Figure 10.28**). Choose either Do Nothing or Execute This Script. To execute a script, you'll have to create a JavaScript.

6. Click Close.

7. Change to the Hand tool to display the check box.

Creating Radio Buttons

While check boxes allow you to choose one or multiple options, radio buttons allow you to select only one item. They're useful when you want to give users mutually exclusive options.

Figure 10.29 Select the Radio Button tool from the Forms toolbar.

To create radio buttons:

1. Choose the Radio Button tool from the Forms toolbar (**Figure 10.29**).

2. Drag to draw the field on the page.

   The Radio Button Properties dialog box appears.

   In the Radio Button Properties dialog box, there are four tabs to choose from: General, Appearance, Options, and Actions.

3. In the dialog box, choose the General tab and name the field, and (if you like) type a brief description in the Tooltip text box. Specify settings in the Common Properties area.

4. Specify settings in the General, Appearance, and Actions panes as you did in previous tasks.

5. On the Options tab, choose a button style from the pop-up menu (**Figure 10.30**). Also enter a value in the Export Value text box (the default will be Yes), which is the answer to the question that the radio button poses (for example, the form may ask users if they are registered voters). Also choose whether the button is selected by default, and if buttons with the same name and value are selected simultaneously.

6. Click Close.

7. Change to the Hand tool to display the check box.

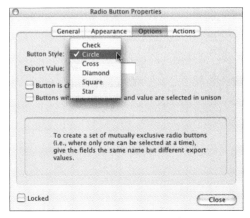

Figure 10.30 Pick a style for your radio button.

✔ Tip

■ To create a *set* of exclusive radio buttons (the user can choose only one option from among one or more sets of radio buttons), you need to assign all the radio button fields the same name but different export values.

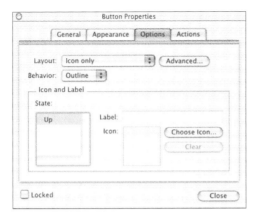

Figure 10.31 On the Options tab, choose a button layout and behavior.

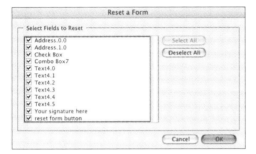

Figure 10.32 Use the Add button in the Actions tab to open the Reset a Form dialog box.

Setting Advanced Form Options

When you have the basic form elements in place, you can assign to them any number of actions and tasks. You can have your forms not only collect information, but also perform some analysis on that information and send it wherever it's needed. You can use a button field to create a *reset form button,* which returns all of the fields in the form to their default settings. You can also export form data information into a spreadsheet program.

To create a reset form button:

1. Select the Button tool from the Forms toolbar.

2. Drag to create a field for the reset form button.

   When you release the mouse button, the Button Properties dialog box opens.

3. In the Button Properties dialog box, choose the General tab to name the field, and (if you like) type a brief description in the Tooltip text box. Click the Appearance tab to change the border color, background color, line thickness, and line style of the button.

4. Click the Options tab. Choose a button layout and behavior from the pop-up menu (**Figure 10.31**). Set any of the other options you would like for this button.

5. Click the Actions tab. Select a trigger (I chose Mouse Up), and choose Reset a Form from the Select Action pop-up menu.

6. Click the Add button to open the Reset a Form dialog box (**Figure 10.32**). Choose which fields you want to reset.

   You can choose Select All or Deselect All so you can specify only certain fields in your form that will reset.

(continues on next page)

SETTING ADVANCED FORM OPTIONS

7. Click OK to return to the Actions tab of the Button Properties dialog box.

The Reset a Form action shows up in the Actions list box.

8. Click the Close button.

9. Choose the Hand tool to view the button (**Figure 10.33**).

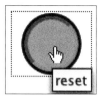

Figure 10.33 The Hand tool lets you view your new button.

✔ Tip

■ You can change the look of a button at any time by double-clicking it with the Form tool and then clicking the Appearance tab of the Field Properties dialog box.

To export form data:

1. Choose Advanced > Forms > Export Data from Form (**Figure 10.34**).

The Export Form Data As dialog box opens.

2. Choose a destination for the form data, type a name for the data, and click Save (**Figure 10.35**).

✔ Tip

■ The information you export from a form has a smaller file size than the form because it doesn't contain all the form-field information. This way, you can archive the file or send it via email.

You can import data that appears on several forms, such as names and addresses, from one form. Then, you can use that imported data to quickly fill in other forms and save yourself a lot of time. To do this, use the Import Form Data command from the Forms submenu of the Advanced menu. Then locate the data file and select it to import the data.

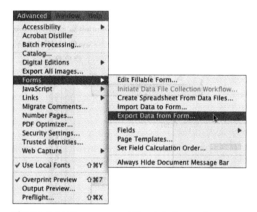

Figure 10.34 You can export the data from a form.

Figure 10.35 Enter a destination and name to save the exported data.

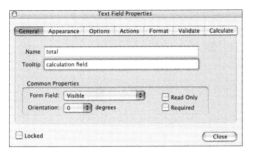

Figure 10.36 On the General tab, give the field a name and a tool tip description.

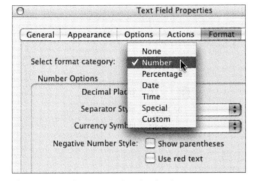

Figure 10.37 Choose Number for the format category.

Using Calculated Fields

Acrobat 7 lets you define a field that displays the results of a calculation using data from two or more other fields. Suppose that your form has several fields in which a user enters dollar amounts. You can define a Total field to display the sum of the entered values. The simplest calculations (Sum, Product, Average, Minimum, and Maximum) are available only for text fields and combo boxes. For more complex procedures, you can use JavaScript to define a custom calculation script. A discussion of JavaScript is beyond the scope of this book, but you can get help from other sources. Acrobat's Help menu offers some assistance; just enter "JavaScript" in the Search field. A more comprehensive source is John Deubert's *Extending Acrobat Forms with JavaScript* (Adobe Press, 2003), or you can download the "Acrobat JavaScript Object Reference" from the Adobe Web site (www.adobe.com).

To create a calculated field:

1. Select the Text Field tool from the Forms toolbar.

2. Drag a box to create the calculation field. When you release the mouse button, the Text Field Properties dialog box opens.

3. On the General tab (**Figure 10.36**), enter a name and tool tip description. Set options on the Appearance tab as well.

4. Click the Format tab. Choose Number from the Select Format Category pop-up menu (**Figure 10.37**).

(continues on next page)

5. Enter the number of decimal places, how you want the numbers separated, the currency style, and how you want a negative number displayed.

6. Click the Calculate tab.

7. Select the second radio button from the top and choose Sum *from the pop-up menu.* Click the Pick button to choose which fields you want to calculate.

This brings up the Field Selection dialog box (**Figure 10.38**).

The Field Selection dialog box lists all of the created fields, buttons, signatures, check boxes, and radio buttons in the PDF document. Choose which fields are to be calculated by checking or unchecking specific fields.

8. Click OK to return to the Text Field Properties dialog box.

9. Click Close to set this field as a calculated field.

Now when you enter amounts in the selected fields, Acrobat calculates the sum of the values in those fields.

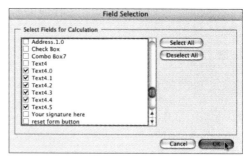

Figure 10.38 Specify which fields are to be calculated by checking fields.

About Advanced Features

Acrobat offers many advanced features for forms. Here's just a basic explanation of what they can do to get you familiar with them:

Create Spreadsheet from Data Files: Data collected in FDF (Form Data Format, an Adobe-specific format) and XML formats can be organized and exported into a spreadsheet, and you can then work on the data in a spreadsheet program such as Microsoft Excel.

Import Data to Form: Import FDF, XML, TXT, XFD, and XFDF formats into a PDF format. Each row must be tab-delineated so that Acrobat can create columns to organize the data.

Export Data to Form: This feature lets you export data information into a TXT, XFDF, FDF, or XML file.

Initiate Data File Collection Workflow: This feature lets you distribute a form and collect data from the forms via email.

Using Designer to Create Your Form (Windows)

If you have Adobe Acrobat 7.0 Professional for Windows, you can create forms using drawing tools similar to those you find in many graphics programs. This version of Acrobat ships with Adobe Designer 7.0, a powerful forms tool that lets you create forms from scratch. You can use Designer to create forms for a server, include calculations, and make forms accessible for those with low vision and mobility impairments. You can access Adobe Designer by choosing Start > All Programs > Adobe Designer 7.0 (**Figure 10.39**).

When you first open Adobe Designer 7.0, the Welcome Screen is displayed. From the Welcome Screen, choose one of these options: New Form, New from Template, Open Form, Quick Start Tutorial, Explore Sample Forms, or What's New. To familiarize yourself with the tool, use the tutorial to create a general office survey form, such as a reminder notice for payment, or go to the more advanced tutorial to create a purchase order form (**Figure 10.40**). If you are looking for more specific types of forms, go directly to the Adobe Designer Help and choose a Quick Step.

When using Designer to create a form, you can choose an existing form or a custom form, or use a standard template to design the layout of your form. In the Designer main window, you're presented with the Layout Editor, which is the area where you will design your forms.

Figure 10.39 Use Adobe Designer to create form designs and layouts.

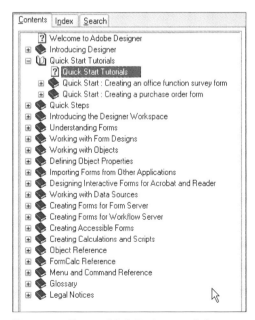

Figure 10.40 The tutorials in Designer can help you create a form design fast.

Figure 10.41 Choose a starting point for your form.

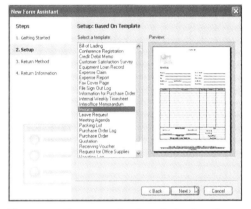

Figure 10.42 You can create a form design from the default templates shown in this dialog box.

Figure 10.43 When you click the Finish button, you can see your new form.

To create a standard form design with Designer:

1. Choose File > New.

   This will launch the New Form Assistant.

   You can't access any of the menus or menu items if the Welcome Screen is still onscreen. If it is, close it and then choose File > New. If you don't want the Welcome Screen to come up each time you launch Designer, uncheck the Always Show This Dialog radio button in the Welcome Screen.

2. Choose from these options: New Blank Form, Based on a Template, Import a PDF Document, or Import a Word Document. (For this exercise, I chose Based on a Template.) Click the Next button (**Figure 10.41**).

3. Pick from the list of default templates. (I chose Invoice.) Click the Next button (**Figure 10.42**).

4. On the next screen of the New Form Assistant, choose a return method: Fill Then Submit, Fill Then Submit/Print, Fill Then Print, or Print. (I chose Fill Then Submit.) Click the Next button.

5. Enter the return information, which will be the return email address. Click the Finish button.

   Your newly created form appears in the main window (**Figure 10.43**).

6. Choose File > Save As to launch the Save As dialog box. Enter a filename, location, and file type; then click the Save button to save your file.

   Open this file in Acrobat to enter the form field information.

✔ Tip

■ Once you create a form in Adobe Designer, you can edit the form fields only in Designer, not in Acrobat.

Adding Multimedia to PDFs

A few years ago, you needed a doctorate in Macromedia Director to create anything remotely akin to multimedia. Now more and more people are using Acrobat to accomplish the same things, such as creating a presentation or a slideshow.

Acrobat provides a simple way for you to add buttons, movies, sounds, and other multimedia components to PDF files. You can create multimedia elements in many programs, from QuarkXPress to Adobe InDesign, Photoshop, or Illustrator, and include them in your PDF documents.

Creating Buttons

Buttons are important elements of any multimedia display. The user clicks a button to
trigger any number of actions—playing a
movie, going to a certain PDF document
page, opening a file in another application,
playing a sound, or linking to a Web page.
Any element can be used as a button.
Acrobat's Link tool makes the process
relatively effortless.

To turn an existing element into a button:

1. Open a PDF file that contains words
   or graphics that you want to turn into
   a button.

2. Choose the Link tool from the Advanced
   Editing toolbar (**Figure 11.1**).

3. Drag a rectangle around the object you
   want to use as a button.

   When you release the mouse button,
   the Create Link dialog box appears
   (**Figure 11.2**).

4. Choose a link type.

   I chose Visible Rectangle from the Link
   Type pop-up menu.

5. Choose a highlight style.

   I chose Invert from the Highlight Style
   pop-up menu.

6. Choose the type of action you'd like
   the button to perform from the Link
   Action area.

   For this example, I've chosen the Go to
   a Page View link action, which lets you
   choose a specific page to link to the
   button. You'll learn more about actions
   later in this chapter. For information on
   adding an action to a form field, see
   Chapter 10, "Forms."

Figure 11.1 You'll find the Link tool on the Advanced
Editing toolbar.

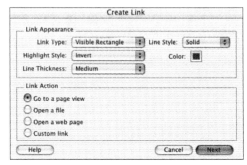

Figure 11.2 After you draw with the Link tool, the
Create Link dialog box appears.

Figure 11.3 The Create Go to View dialog box opens.

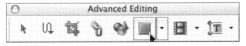

Figure 11.4 Choose the Button tool from the Advanced Editing toolbar.

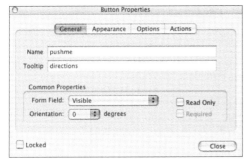

Figure 11.5 The Button Properties dialog box lets you control how your button will look and perform.

7. Click the Next button.

This launches the Create Go to View dialog box (**Figure 11.3**). Use the scroll bars (to move down or up a page), the Pages pane (to jump to a different page), and the magnification tools (to zoom in or out on a page) to make the page look the way you want. When finished, click the Set Link button to complete the link action. To activate the link, use the Hand tool and click on the button.

To add a button to a PDF file:

1. Find the place in the document where you want to put your button, and choose the Button tool from the Advanced Editing toolbar (**Figure 11.4**).

2. In the document, drag to create the area in which the button will be placed.

When you release the mouse button, the Button Properties dialog box appears (**Figure 11.5**).

3. Choose the General tab in the Button Properties dialog box.

4. Name the button and enter text for a tool tip if you wish. (A tool tip appears when you let your cursor rest on the button.) Specify whether you want the button to be visible and choose the button's orientation.

5. Click the Appearance tab. Enter a border color/thickness/line style, fill color, and font size/type/color.

6. Choose the Options tab.

(continues on next page)

CREATING BUTTONS

7. Choose Icon Only from the Layout pop-up menu.

This will display a picture of a button.

You could also choose one of the other items from the pop-up menu: Label Only, Icon Top/Label Bottom, Label Top/Icon Bottom, Icon Left/Label Right, Label Left/Icon Right, or Label Over Icon.

8. Choose a style from the Behavior pop-up menu.

I chose Push, which shows a picture looking like a button you push inward.

9. Pick a state for the button, such as Up, which shows how the button looks before anyone clicks it.

You can also enter a label name and choose an icon for the button. For this example, I left those areas blank.

10. Choose the Actions tab in the Button Properties dialog box.

11. Select a trigger and an action from the pop-up menus.

I chose Mouse Up (from the Select Trigger menu) and Go to a Page View (from the Select Action menu).

12. Click the Add button.

In my example, this added the Go to a Page View action and launched the Create Go to View dialog box (**Figure 11.6**).

13. Use the scroll bars and magnification tools to go to the page and create the view you wish. Click the Set Link button to set this action, then click the Close button.

When you switch to the Hand tool, the button displays in its up state (**Figure 11.7**). Clicking the button displays its down state (**Figure 11.8**) and triggers the event connected with the button (**Figure 11.9**).

Figure 11.6 The Create Go to View dialog box opens.

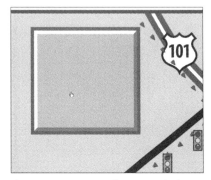

Figure 11.7 You can see the up state before you click the button.

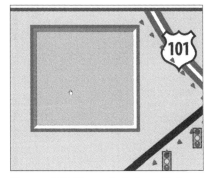

Figure 11.8 Clicking on the button with the Hand tool displays the down state.

Figure 11.9 The event that was connected to the button is triggered. In this case, clicking the button takes you to a specific page of the PDF.

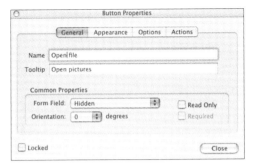

Figure 11.10 You can enter a name and a tool tip in the General tab of the Button Properties dialog box.

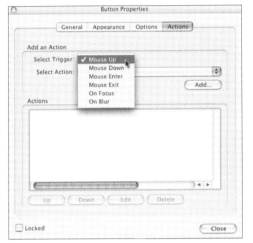

Figure 11.11 Choose a trigger from the Select Trigger pop-up menu in the Actions tab of the Button Properties dialog box.

Adding Actions

The ability to add actions is a powerful feature in Acrobat that lets you make your PDF interactive. For instance, by clicking a button you can go directly to a Web page on the Internet, or you can set an action to link one part of a document to another. You can add actions to links, bookmarks, form fields, media clips, and pages. You have a variety of action types from which to choose: Execute a Menu Item, Go to a Page View, Import Form Data, Open a File, Open a Web Link, Play a Sound, Play Media, Read an Article, Reset a Form, Run a JavaScript, Set Layer Visibility, Show/Hide a Field, and Submit a Form.

To create an action that opens a file:

1. In a PDF document, choose the Button tool from the Forms toolbar.

2. Click and drag in the area in which you'd like to create a button that can open a file.

   When you release the mouse button, the Button Properties dialog box appears.

3. Enter a name, type text for a tool tip if desired, and adjust any of the common properties that you want in the General tab (**Figure 11.10**).

4. Set the way you want the button to look in the Appearance tab.

   I am creating an invisible button with no border or fill color.

5. In the Options tab, set a layout, behavior, and state for the button.

6. Select the Actions tab to add your action to the button.

7. Choose a trigger for the action from the Select Trigger pop-up menu (**Figure 11.11**).

   I chose the Mouse Up trigger.

(continues on next page)

8. Choose an action from the Select Action pop-up menu.

   For this exercise, I chose Open a File.

9. Click the Add button.

   The Select File to Open dialog box appears.

10. Choose the file you want to open with this action by clicking the Select button.

    This launches the Specify Open Preference dialog box (**Figure 11.12**).

11. Choose how you want the file to be opened (Window Set by User Preference, New Window, or Existing Window). Window Set by User Preference means that the file will open according to the settings on the computer of the person opening the file.

12. Click the OK button, which takes you back to the Button Properties dialog box. Click the Close button.

    Now, when you click the Hand tool over the button area, the file you've chosen will open.

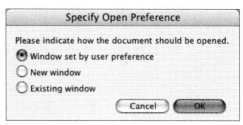

Figure 11.12 The Specify Open Preference dialog box lets you indicate how you want the file to be opened.

Figure 11.13 Click the Add button to include a file in your slideshow.

Creating a Slideshow with Acrobat

One of the less well-known features of Acrobat is its capacity to create a slideshow presentation. What is really fantastic about using Acrobat to do a presentation is that you can send it to anyone via the Internet. For instance, artists can create slideshows of their artwork so that they have a visual gallery for reference. You can create an art gallery, photo gallery, or business presentation with charts, graphs, and other features.

To create a gallery slide show with Acrobat:

1. Choose File > Create PDF > From Multiple Files.

   This launches the Create PDF from Multiple Documents dialog box.

   You can import Adobe PDF files, BMP, GIF, HTML, JPEG, JPEG 200, PCX, PICT, PNG, PostScript/EPS, Text, and TIFF files into Acrobat.

2. Click the Choose button in the Add Files area.

   This launches the Open dialog box.

3. Click the Add button to add a file (**Figure 11.13**).

   Repeat steps 2 and 3 until you have all the files you want in your slideshow. You can arrange the files here or in the Pages pane within Acrobat. I find it easier to rearrange from the Pages pane since you can work with the pages in thumbnail view.

4. Click OK to create the PDF with multiple files for your slideshow.

   Save the slideshow in Acrobat.

(continues on next page)

5. Choose Edit > Preferences/Acrobat > Preferences (Ctrl+K/Command+K).

The Preferences dialog box appears.

6. Choose Full Screen from the list on the left side of the dialog box.

7. In the Full Screen Navigation section, check the Advance Every *x* Seconds check box and type a value in the text box (**Figure 11.14**).

This section also lets you choose how users advance the slides, whether to show a navigation bar, and what will happen at the end of the presentation.

8. In the Full Screen Appearance section, choose a transition style from the Default Transition pop-up menu (**Figure 11.15**).

9. From the Mouse Cursor pop-up menu, choose Always Visible, Always Hidden, or Hidden After Delay to specify how you want the mouse pointer to appear.

10. Choose a background color for the slideshow, then click OK to accept these changes. Remember to save your file with these Full Screen preferences.

11. Choose Window > Full Screen View (Ctrl+L/Command+L).

This will run your slide show with the preferences you selected (**Figure 11.16**).

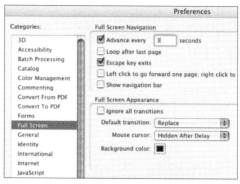

Figure 11.14 Enter the number of seconds you want each slide to remain on screen.

Figure 11.15 Choose a transition style for your slideshow.

Figure 11.16 Choose Full Screen View to run your slideshow.

Figure 11.17 Choose the Movie tool from the Advanced Editing toolbar.

Figure 11.18 The Add Movie dialog box opens.

Figure 11.19 Select a movie and click the Select button.

Adding Sounds or Movies to PDFs

Sounds, whether they are music or recorded explanations that enhance the viewer's understanding of a document, can add greatly to the viewer's experience. A movie can illustrate a procedure for instructional purposes or merely amuse the viewer. You can use the Link tool not only to create a button, as described earlier in this chapter, but also to add multimedia clips to a PDF. You also can use the Movie tool to define a clickable area that triggers the playing of a clip.

To add a multimedia clip with the Movie tool:

1. In an open PDF document, choose the Movie tool from the Advanced Editing toolbar (**Figure 11.17**).

2. Drag a rectangle in the location on your document where you want the clickable area, or *hot spot*.

   When you release the mouse button, the Add Movie dialog box appears (**Figure 11.18**).

3. To use a clip from your hard disk, click the Choose button next to the Location text box.

   The Select Movie File dialog box appears.

4. Select a sound or movie clip, and click the Select button (**Figure 11.19**).

(continues on next page)

5. Check the Snap or Embed options as well as the Poster settings in the Add Movie dialog box, and click OK.

6. Switch to the Hand tool, and click the hot spot to see your movie clip (**Figure 11.20**).

To delete a multimedia clip from a PDF document:

1. With the Movie tool, click the border of the clip to select it.

2. Press the Backspace/Delete key.

✔ Tip

■ Be wary of using any movie or sound that you find on the Web. You need to check the copyright status of movies and sounds, and give appropriate recognition to the owners.

Figure 11.20 Once you click on the movie with the Hand tool, the movie will play.

Giving Users Control of Multimedia Presentations

Many multimedia presentations are *immersive*—that is, the buttons, menus, and controls within the presentation itself control movement of the slides, slide transitions, and any special effects or sounds. In fact, many times the presentation prevents the viewer from accessing the standard menus and commands that they're accustomed to using in other software. So, you may want to provide options to compensate.

A multiple-page document, for example, will need navigation buttons so viewers can go to the following and preceding pages. A Quit or Exit button can be useful. If you have a main menu or table of contents, you might also want to include a button on each page that takes you back to those areas.

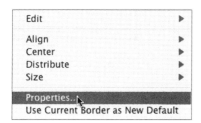

Figure 11.21 Choose Properties from the movie's contextual menu.

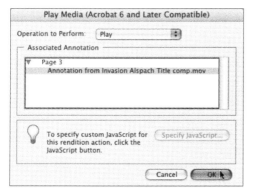

Figure 11.22 Choose the movie you want to insert from the list.

Using Page Actions with Movies

In this section, you set up a movie to play automatically when you view a certain page in a document.

To create a movie that plays automatically:

1. Follow the steps in the task "To add a multimedia clip with the Movie tool" to select and set up a movie to play in a document.

2. With the Movie tool, right-click/Ctrl-click on the movie box to bring up the contextual menu. Choose Properties from this menu (**Figure 11.21**).

   The Multimedia Properties dialog box appears.

3. Choose the Page Enter option from the Select Trigger pop-up menu.

4. Choose Play Media from the Select Action pop-up menu.

5. Click the Add button.

6. Choose the movie from the list by clicking on it, then click OK (**Figure 11.22**).

7. Click the Close button to save this action.

8. Open the Pages pane and choose a different page using the Hand tool.

9. Click on the page in which you created the movie.

   When you go to that page, the movie will play automatically.

CATALOG, INDEXES, AND SEARCHES

Acrobat includes a handy feature called Acrobat Catalog, which creates indexes of PDF files. These indexes save you time when you're looking up a word or words within a PDF or a collection of PDFs. To find a word in an unindexed PDF, you have to use the Find command, which laboriously works its way through a document, testing every single word.

When you process a PDF with Catalog, the program creates a database, listing the location of every word in the document. In other words, all the finding is done ahead of time, so when you need to look up a word, its location is already stored in the index. To look up a word in an indexed document, you use the Search command, which is much more powerful than the Find command.

You can use Catalog to create an index of a single PDF, a folder of PDF documents, or all the PDFs on a disk. Catalog allows you to search across several indexed documents at the same time.

Getting Ready to Index

You can use Catalog to create an index file of a few PDF documents or a whole group of files. Catalog organizes your PDF files in groups that can be searched even over a large network.

Because the index keeps track of the locations of words and documents at the time you indexed them, you must devote some effort to setting up your documents before you start the indexing process. If the index is to be used in a cross-platform environment, you also need to take into account the requirements of the different operating systems. An exhaustive description of all the considerations for building an index is beyond the scope of this book, but you'll find several pages of suggestions and requirements in Adobe's documentation.

To prepare documents for indexing:

◆ Searching goes faster in small documents, so think about breaking your documents into separate PDFs by section or chapter.

◆ Bring your documents as close to a state of perfection as possible: add all bookmarks and links, create all form fields, enter information (including document titles) into the Document Summary dialog box.

◆ Make sure that all file and folder names will translate properly across platforms, if your index will be used in a multiplatform environment. To be absolutely safe, rename all files according to the MS-DOS file-naming limitation of 8 characters or fewer.

◆ Gather all of the documents to be indexed into a single folder. Adobe Catalog will store the index that it produces in this folder. Documents can be nested within subfolders of this folder, but you must keep documents in the same folder hierarchy after indexing is complete; otherwise, searches will be unable to find them.

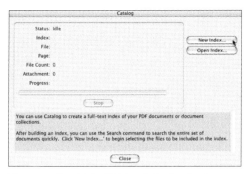

Figure 12.1 The Adobe Catalog dialog box is where you start creating or accessing indexes.

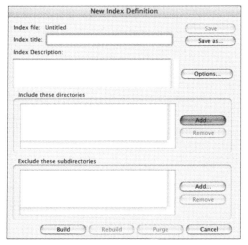

Figure 12.2 The New Index Definition dialog box contains text boxes for basic index information, such as index name, description, and directories in the index.

Figure 12.3 On the Macintosh, select the desired directories and then click Choose. In the Windows dialog box, click the folder icon to display subdirectories.

Creating Indexes

When your files are finished, named, and stored in a folder, you're ready to start using Acrobat Catalog to build your index.

To create an index:

1. Choose Catalog from the Advanced menu. The Catalog dialog box appears.

2. Click the New Index button (**Figure 12.1**). The New Index Definition dialog box opens (**Figure 12.2**).

3. Type the index title and description in the appropriate text boxes.

4. Click the Add button in the Include These Directories /Exclude These Subdirectories areas to open the Add Include/Exclude Directory dialog box.

5. Navigate to the files you want to include in your index. To include a selected directory, click Choose or click the folder icons (Windows) or the Open button (Mac OS) to access subdirectories (**Figure 12.3**).

   You return to the New Index Definition dialog box. The directory names appear in the Include These Directories list. Click Remove to delete any folders you've chosen by mistake.

6. To omit subfolders that you don't want to index, repeat steps 4 and 5 but this time click the Add button next to the Exclude These Subdirectories list box to open the Exclude Directory dialog box.

(continues on next page)

7. Click the Options button in the New Index Definition dialog to set additional options for the index.

The Options dialog box opens (**Figure 12.4**). You can exclude numbers and certain words for quicker indexing, and set word options, such as specifying XMP fields and structure tags to be indexed for searches. Click OK after you make your selections, and you return to the New Index Definition dialog box.

8. Click the Build button to start the indexing.

The Save Index File dialog box opens (**Figure 12.5**).

9. Choose a location in which to store the index, type a filename (or accept the default name), and click Save.

You'll see the progress of the index in the Catalog dialog box; keep in mind that this progress may be very slow (**Figure 12.6**). The index is saved as a .pdx file.

10. Click the Close button when the index is complete.

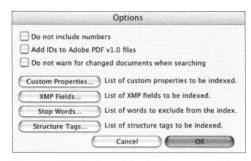

Figure 12.4 The Options dialog box lets you exclude certain elements to minimize index size.

Figure 12.5 Type a name for the new index and choose a location in which to store it.

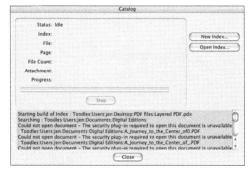

Figure 12.6 You can watch the progress of the index building in the Catalog dialog box.

CREATING INDEXES

✔ Tips

■ In the Options dialog box, you can specify "stop words" that should be omitted from the index. For example, in creating a searchable index for this book, it would make sense to exclude the terms "PDF" and "Acrobat," since they appear on nearly every page and are therefore useless as search items. By removing such items, you can greatly reduce the size of the catalog file without limiting its utility.

■ The Catalog feature indexes only folders of PDF files. If you want to index the contents of an individual PDF file, you must create a folder and place that PDF file into it.

■ The size of the index file created by Catalog can be very large, up to 40 percent of the total size of the PDF files being indexed. This can be an issue if you are distributing a CD containing PDF files along with their index; you need to allow room for the index file.

■ When you distribute an index along with a set of PDF files, the two files must maintain the same relative position in the target disk's hierarchy. If the PDF files and their index are in the same folder, they must remain together in the same folder when you move them to another disk.

CREATING INDEXES

Making Changes to Indexes

Occasionally, if you add documents to your collection, you will want to catalog them and add the results to the collection's index. Similarly, if documents are no longer in your directory, it's a good idea to remove them from the index so that Acrobat doesn't try to search for something that isn't there.

For speed in indexing, when you change an index, Catalog will add only the differences between the new and old information to the existing index.

To add to an index:

1. Choose Catalog from the Advanced menu.

   The Catalog dialog box opens.

2. Click the Open Index button to open the index you want to alter.

   The Open dialog box appears.

3. Select the index you want to open, and click Open.

   The Index Definition dialog box appears.

4. Click the Add button next to the Include These Directories list box (**Figure 12.7**).

5. In the resulting dialog box, add the directories that contain the new material, and exclude any subdirectories.

6. In the Index Definition dialog, click the Save button to retain the index file's original name or the Save As button to rename the file.

7. Click the Rebuild button to add the new information to the index.

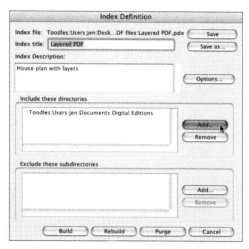

Figure 12.7 Choose the directories that you want to include in the index.

To remove directories from an index:

1. Choose Catalog from the Advanced menu.

   The Catalog dialog box opens.

2. Click the Open Index button to open the index you want to change.

   The Open dialog box appears.

3. Select the index you want to open, and click Open.

   The Index Definition dialog box appears.

4. Select a directory to delete and click the Remove button next to the Include These Directories list box.

5. Click the Save button to retain the index file's original name or the Save As button to rename the file.

6. Click the Rebuild button to remove the information from the index.

✔ Tip

■ The Purge button in the New Index Definition dialog box can be helpful. If you've made major changes in an indexed directory, purging the index rebuilds it entirely. Invalid entries from the original index are deleted. Purging reduces the overall size of the index and slightly increases search speed, depending on the number of documents and words cataloged.

MAKING CHANGES TO INDEXES

Searching Indexes

Figure 12.8 Use Search to find specific contents in your PDF document.

After a PDF has been indexed with the Catalog utility, you can look up information in it by using the Search command, which is more powerful and flexible than the Find command. The Find command can do a basic search in your PDF document, but the Search command can do far more in-depth and advanced work. You can search the contents of form fields; search for words that are related to, or sound like, the words in the Search box; or construct searches with Boolean operators (which let you search for exact words and alternate words, or exclude words). I'll cover some basic searches to get you started. To learn about more complex searches, consult the Acrobat documentation.

Figure 12.9 Enter search words or phrases in the Search PDF dialog box.

To perform a search:

1. Choose Edit > Search (Ctrl+Shift+F/ Command+Shift+F) or click the Search button in the File toolbar (**Figure 12.8**).

   The Search PDF dialog box appears (**Figure 12.9**).

2. Type the word or words that you want to search for in the text box at the top of the dialog box.

3. Click the check boxes to set search options, such as Whole Words Only.

4. Click the Use Advanced Search Options link at the bottom of the dialog box.

   New options, including the Look In drop-down menu, will appear at the top of the dialog.

5. In the Look In drop-down menu, select Select Indexes.

   Acrobat will display the Index Selection dialog box.

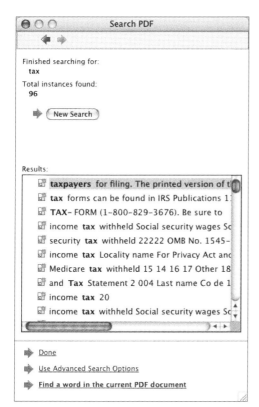

Figure 12.10 The results of the search are shown in the Results list box.

6. Click the Add button to add an index to the list of indexes to be searched. Acrobat will present you with a dialog box where you can navigate to the index file you want to add to the list and click Open.

7. Click the OK button to dismiss the dialog box. Note that the Look In menu will now read Currently Selected Indexes.

8. Click the Search button to start the search.

When the search is finished, the Results area of the Search PDF dialog box appears and displays all the documents that contain matches for the search criteria (**Figure 12.10**). If you want to do another search, click the New Search button.

9. Select the document you want to view and double-click it to open it.

The document will automatically jump to the page with the search results highlighted.

Setting Catalog Preferences

Acrobat Catalog is highly customizable; you can change several parameters in the Catalog Preferences dialog box. For instance, you can enable logging or allow indexing on separate drives. But Adobe strongly recommends that unless you're sure about what you're doing, resist the temptation to fiddle with the default settings. With that warning, I'll provide a brief introduction to adjusting Catalog to your liking. If you'd like more information, refer to Adobe's documentation.

To change Catalog preferences:

1. Choose Preferences from the File menu (Windows) or from the Acrobat menu (Mac).

   Then choose Catalog from the list on the left of the Preferences dialog box (**Figure 12.11**).

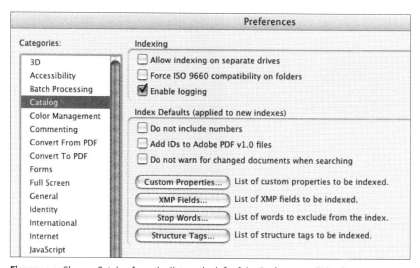

Figure 12.11 Choose Catalog from the list on the left of the Preferences dialog box.

2. Change any of the areas to your preference:

▲ **Indexing** options allow indexing on separate drives, force ISO 9660 compatibility on folders (so you don't have to rename a PDF to fit the 8-character limitation of MS-DOS file naming), and enable logging, which might help someone troubleshoot an index gone wrong.

▲ **Index Defaults** settings include Do Not Include Numbers (this setting can significantly reduce the file size of indexes); Add IDs to Adobe PDF v1.0 Files (the older version of Adobe PDF files did not include an automatic identification as the later versions do; ID numbers are needed when Mac OS filenames are shortened); and Do Not Warn for Changed Documents when Searching.

▲ **Custom Properties** can be useful if your indexed directories include forms. You can add fields from forms to the indexed items, allowing users to search in those fields. In addition, you can set XMP fields (XMP is information Adobe applications can place in a file to help other Adobe applications, like Illustrator, use that file), stop words (a feature that lets you exclude specific words from an index search), and structure tags.

3. When you finish setting preferences, click OK.

SETTING CATALOG PREFERENCES

13

Paper Capture

Wouldn't it be nice if you could convert all your paper-based documents to PDF format? Then you could archive those documents electronically and distribute them via email or CD-ROM. Acrobat provides a plug-in that helps you do just that.

Acrobat lets you scan in documents that contain images, text, columns, and more while retaining images, colors, fonts, and other elements. You can make the text editable in case you want to alter it or do searches on it. Acrobat will even help you out by looking for text that may not have been converted correctly in the editable text.

Scanning a Document into Acrobat

To turn a paper document into a PDF, you first have to create an image of it in your computer. The most direct way is to scan the document. You can have Acrobat control the scanning process by using the Import command.

In general, when you install the software that came with your scanner, the installation program will find scanner-capable programs, such as Acrobat, on your computer and install the software that operates the scanner (usually in the form of a plug-in) in each of those programs. Once you have scanned in the image or text, use Acrobat to capture it to make it editable.

When you are scanning documents, keep in mind that the higher the quality of the scan, the larger the resulting image file will be. The trick is getting the best scan for your purposes without ending up with a file that takes up too much space on your hard disk and is slow to manipulate.

Before starting to scan, think carefully about two parameters in your scanning software: color mode and resolution. For the color-mode setting, you'll normally choose grayscale or color. If the document you're scanning was printed in full color, use color. If your document was printed in black ink, choose the grayscale option. Scan color images in grayscale mode if you want to keep down the file size or if the PDF will be printed only on black and white laser printers.

How to Choose a Scanning Resolution

Resolution is the fineness of detail in the scan, measured in dots per inch (dpi). Choose a resolution based on the content of the document and taking into account how you plan to use the PDF. If the document consists only of images that people will read onscreen, a resolution of around 75 dpi is fine. If your document contains text, and you intend to convert the scan into editable text (*captured text*, in Acrobat jargon), you need to scan at a much higher resolution—say, 300 dpi. Line art requires a resolution of approximately 600 dpi.

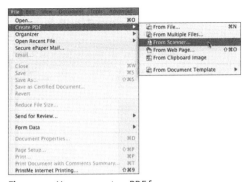

Figure 13.1 You can create a PDF from a scanner.

Figure 13.2 The Create PDF From Scanner dialog box appears for you to choose your scanner.

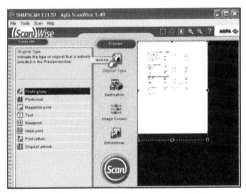

Figure 13.3 Once you click Scan, your scanning software launches.

To scan an image to be captured:

1. Place the document to be scanned face down on the scanner.

2. In Acrobat, choose File > Create PDF > From Scanner (**Figure 13.1**), or click the Create PDF button and choose From Scanner from the pop-up menu.

   The Create PDF From Scanner dialog box appears (**Figure 13.2**).

3. From the Scanner pop-up menu, choose your scanner.

4. Choose single-sided or double-sided from the Scan pop-up menu, depending on the nature of your original.

5. In the Destination pop-up menu, specify whether you want to create a new PDF from the scanned material or add the material to the currently open PDF.

6. Click Scan.

   Your scanner's software launches (**Figure 13.3**).

7. Enter your settings for the type of image or color mode, destination (where to save the file), and resolution.

   continues on next page

SCANNING A DOCUMENT INTO ACROBAT

8. Click the Scan button to start the scan into Acrobat.

   The scan will show the progress as it is scanning (**Figure 13.4**).

9. Click the Done button in the Acrobat Scan Plug-in dialog box when you finish scanning documents (**Figure 13.5**).

   Acrobat converts the image to an untitled PDF document (**Figure 13.6**).

10. Save the file by choosing File > Save As.

✔ Tips

- You can rotate a scanned page in Acrobat by choosing Rotate Pages from the Document menu (Ctrl+Shift+R/ Command+Shift+R). You can rotate specific pages or all pages.

- If the scan has extra space around it, choose the Crop Pages command from the Document menu (Ctrl+Shift+T/ Command+Shift+T). This command lets you crop one or all pages.

Figure 13.4 Watch the progress of your scan.

Figure 13.5 Click the Next button if you are scanning multiple pages.

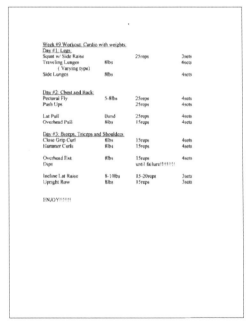

Figure 13.6 Acrobat has converted the image into a PDF document.

Capturing and Editing Images and Text

The PDF that you just created is simply an image file. Even if it contains text, all you have is a picture of text; the file is not recognized by the computer as text and can't be edited, searched, or indexed. To remedy this situation, you need to *capture* the document. This process turns scanned text into editable text and images into stand-alone image objects within the document. (The technical term is optical character recognition, or OCR.) One of the benefits of this conversion is that captured text (as characters) takes up drastically less space than a comparable scan of the same text.

To prepare a document for Paper Capture, you must scan according to these parameters:

◆ 200–600 dpi for black-and-white images (300 usually is best)

◆ 200–400 dpi for color or grayscale images

If you don't follow those specifications, Paper Capture will give you error messages.

✔ Tip

■ If you have large numbers of documents to convert to PDFs, you might consider investing in Adobe's Acrobat Capture program. The industrial-strength version operates as a server application, which several users can access over a network.

Setting Capture Options

As Capture converts text from images into editable text, it needs to know what sort of language and alphabet it should be looking for. You can choose the language in the Paper Capture Settings dialog box. You can also decide how fine you want the resolution of downsampled images (images with decreased number of pixels for a smaller file size) and choose the style of the output, such as formatted text and graphics.

To change Paper Capture settings:

1. Choose Document > Recognize Text Using OCR > Start Capture.

   The Paper Capture dialog box appears.

2. Click the Edit button (**Figure 13.7**).

   The Paper Capture Settings dialog box opens, with the defaults showing (**Figure 13.8**).

3. From the pop-up menus, make choices to specify the language that Capture should look for, the output style, and the resolution of downsampled images.

4. Click OK.

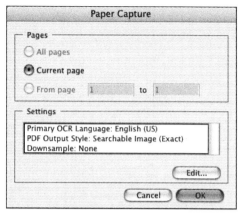

Figure 13.7 Click the Edit button in the Paper Capture dialog box.

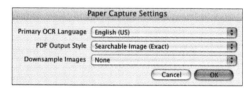

Figure 13.8 The Paper Capture Settings dialog box opens.

SETTING CAPTURE OPTIONS

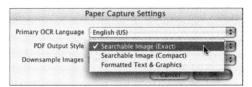

Figure 13.9 Choose the PDF Output Style from the pop-up menu.

Working with Scanned Text

If you want to be able to edit the text you've scanned into Acrobat, you can convert an Adobe PDF to one of three formats:

◆ **Adobe PDF Formatted Text and Graphics,** used for most standard PDF files. It replaces bitmapped text with editable text in fonts that look similar to the ones in the original document.

◆ **PDF Searchable Image (Exact)** retains the bitmapped appearance (a grid of pixels forming text) of the original document. The editable text is supplied on an invisible layer below the bitmap.

◆ **Searchable Image (Compact)** segments the original image to allow different areas to be compressed, sacrificing image quality but resulting in a smaller file.

You can choose a format in the Paper Capture dialog box.

To get to the Paper Capture dialog box:

1. Choose Document > Recognize Text Using OCR > Start Capture.

2. In the Paper Capture dialog box, you can click the Edit button to access the other formats.

3. Choose the PDF Output Style pop-up for all three choices (**Figure 13.9**).

4. Once you make your choice, click OK to return to the Paper Capture dialog box, and from there click OK to start the capture process.

To convert scanned text to editable text:

1. Open the scanned image file, which you saved in PDF format.

2. Choose Document > Recognize Text Using OCR > Start Capture.

   The Paper Capture dialog box appears.

3. Select Current Page.

   If you want to capture more than one page, select either All Pages to capture each page or Specified Range to capture a certain range of page (such as pages 4 through 8).

4. Click OK.

   When the conversion is finished, the document appears in captured form.

Figure 13.10 shows a PDF document before being captured, and **Figure 13.11** shows the same document after being captured. The biggest difference between a PDF before and after being captured is that the background of the scanned document is slightly gray instead of pure white like the background of the converted file. And, of course, you can select and edit text in the captured document.

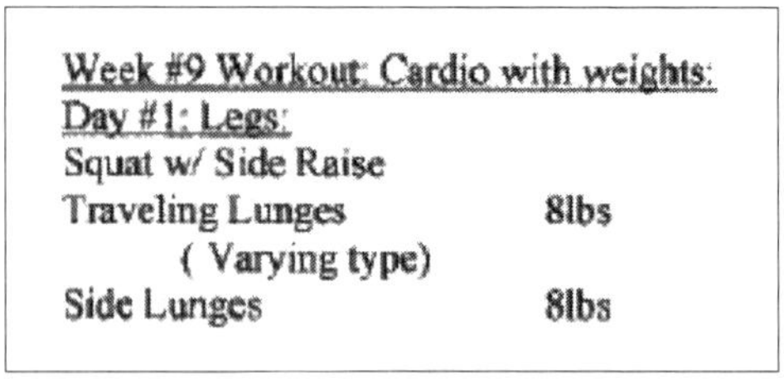

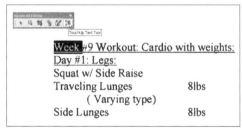

Figure 13.10 The PDF before capture shows pixelized text.

Figure 13.11 After the capture, the text looks like normal text.

Figure 13.12 Use the TouchUp Text tool to edit the captured text.

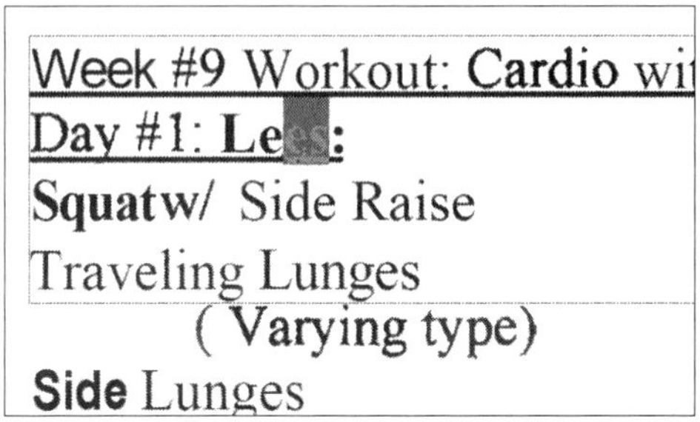

Week #9 Workout: Cardio wi
Day #1: Le‗s:
Squatw/ Side Raise
Traveling Lunges
(Varying type)
Side Lunges

Figure 13.13 Select the text to be edited.

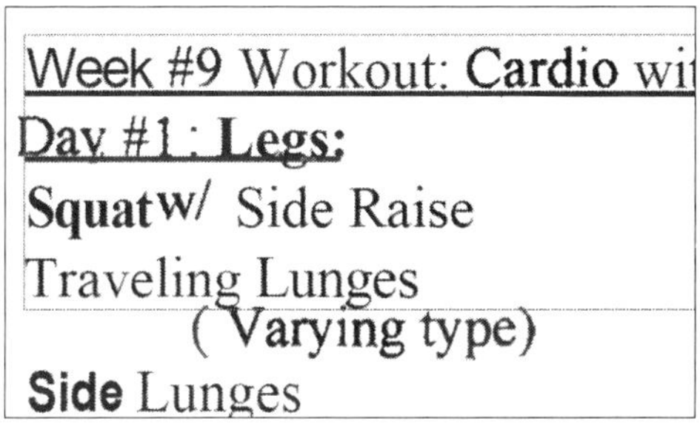

Week #9 Workout: Cardio wi
Day #1: Legs:
Squatw/ Side Raise
Traveling Lunges
(Varying type)
Side Lunges

Figure 13.14 Enter the replacement character or characters.

To edit captured text:

1. Choose the TouchUp Text tool from the toolbar (**Figure 13.12**). If it isn't visible, choose View > Toolbars > Advanced Editing.

2. Click the text you'd like to edit (**Figure 13.13**). Click and drag to edit more letters, double-click on a word to select the whole word, or click and drag over one letter to edit that letter.

   Because the text is now in editable form, you can change letters, spelling, and punctuation by selecting the characters to be changed and typing over them.

3. Type the replacement character(s) (**Figure 13.14**).

4. To continue reading the document, switch back to the Hand tool by choosing it from the toolbar.

Working with Suspects

Occasionally, Acrobat's Capture plug-in has trouble interpreting a word or character. In such cases, Acrobat substitutes what it thinks is correct and marks the word or character as a *suspect*. This section shows you how to review the suspects within a captured PDF.

To find and review suspects:

1. Choose Document > Recognize Text Using OCR > Find All OCR Suspects (**Figure 13.15**).

   The suspect words appear in the Acrobat window, outlined with red rectangles (**Figure 13.16**).

2. Choose Document > Recognize Text Using OCR > Find First OCR Suspect.

   The Find Element dialog box opens (**Figure 13.17**). The first suspect element appears in the middle of the Find Element dialog box.

3. To accept Acrobat's interpretation of the text in the Find Element dialog box, click the Accept and Find button.

   If you don't accept the change to the suspect, you can leave the bitmapped image in place, but you won't be able to edit it later. It is best to accept the interpretation so that Acrobat will transfer the suspect into editable text, and then you can use the TouchUp Text tool to edit the text.

4. Continue until all suspects are addressed.

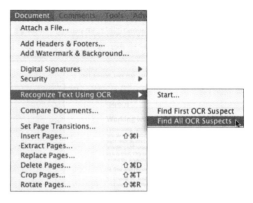

Figure 13.15 You can find one suspect at a time, or all suspects in the captured text.

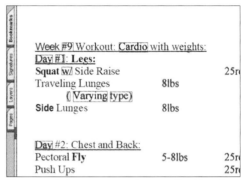

Figure 13.16 The suspect words are outlined in red in the Acrobat window.

Figure 13.17 The Find Element dialog box displays the suspect word.

14

DIGITAL SIGNATURES

The digital signature is becoming the standard for signing important electronic documents and in many environments carries the authority of a handwritten signature. Acrobat offers users the ability to create a digital signature, which is a piece of encrypted data stored in a PDF. It gives you a visual indication that a PDF has been signed. A digital signature can be one of three things: a handwritten name, a logo (or symbol graphic), or text. Not only can you create a digital signature and sign PDF documents digitally, but you can also verify that signature's authenticity.

Creating a Digital ID

In order to sign a document digitally, you first need a digital ID.

To create a digital ID:

1. Choose Advanced > Security Settings (**Figure 14.1**).

   This opens the Security Settings dialog box.

2. Choose Digital IDs in the listing on the left, then click the Add ID button (**Figure 14.2**).

   This launches the Add Digital ID wizard (**Figure 14.3**).

3. Click the Create a Self-Signed Digital ID radio button, and then click the Next button.

Figure 14.1 Choose Advanced > Security Settings.

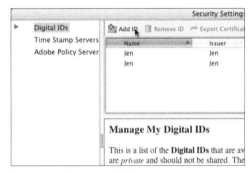

Figure 14.2 Click the Add ID button.

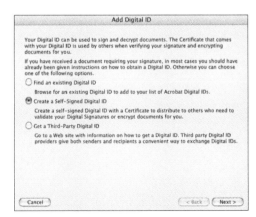

Figure 14.3 The first page of the Add Digital ID wizard asks you to choose one of three options.

CREATING A DIGITAL ID

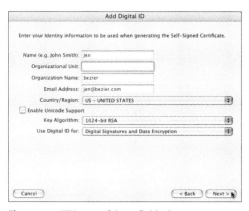

Figure 14.4 Fill in any of these fields that you want to use with your Digital ID.

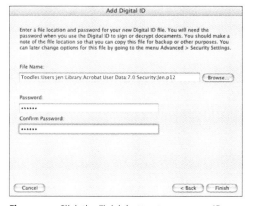

Figure 14.5 Click the Finish button to save your ID.

4. Enter your identity information in the Add Digital ID window shown in **Figure 14.4**; then click the Next button.

5. In the next window, use the default file location or click Browse if you want to choose a different location.

6. Enter a password, and confirm that password in the same window (**Figure 14.5**). Then click the Finish button.

   Your new self-signed Digital ID is saved in the Security Settings dialog box. Dismiss the box by clicking the Close button.

✔ Tips

- If you always use the same ID and want to set it as the default, select the ID by clicking on it in the Security Settings dialog box, click the Set Default menu, and choose from the three options in the menu.

- On Windows computers, you don't need to set a password as you do on a Macintosh, because Acrobat uses Windows' Certificate Security Method, which you use when you log into Windows.

CREATING A DIGITAL ID

Handling Digital Signatures

Self-Sign Security is Acrobat's default signature handler—software that creates and authenticates signatures. This software requires you, the signer, to create a digital ID that will be used to create and later verify signatures you place on PDF files. Among other things, the digital ID includes a password that you must provide when signing a document.

If you want to switch to a different signature handler, you'll need to adjust Acrobat to use that software as the default handler in the Security preferences. Typically, this is the task of an IT department.

Acrobat supports Microsoft's code signing and digital security with MS CAPI (Microsoft's cryptographic service provider).

To add a handwritten signature or logo to a profile:

1. Scan your signature or logo into a bitmap graphics program (such as Adobe Photoshop) or use a program like Adobe Illustrator to create your signature or logo and then save it as a PDF.

2. Choose Edit/Acrobat > Preferences (Ctrl+K/Command+K) to open the General pane of the Preferences window.

3. Select Security in the list on the left, and click the New button in the Appearance area (**Figure 14.6**).

   This brings up the Configure Signature Appearance dialog box.

4. Type a title for the signature, and click the Imported Graphic radio button.

5. Click the File button (**Figure 14.7**) to find your PDF file.

   This opens the Select Picture dialog box. Click the Browse button to launch the Open dialog box.

6. Navigate to the PDF file of the signature that you saved, and click the Select button. You return to the Select Picture dialog box.

7. Click OK.

   The Configure Signature Appearance dialog box displays a preview of the graphic (**Figure 14.8**).

8. Click OK to close the Configure Signature Appearance dialog box.

9. Click OK to accept your changes and close Preferences.

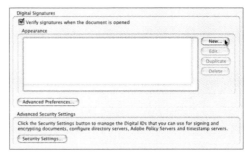

Figure 14.6 Click the New button in the Appearance area of Security Preferences.

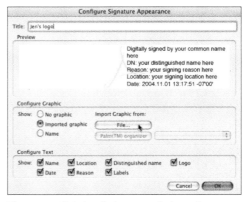

Figure 14.7 Click the File button to find your image.

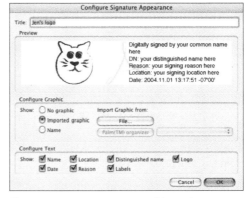

Figure 14.8 You can see your graphic preview.

✔ Tip

■ In the Configure Text section of the Configure Signature Appearance dialog box, you can choose to have additional information displayed along with your signature. This information includes the date; your reason for signing the document (such as needing an approval signature); the location of the saved digital ID; and a distinguished name (such as Doctor, Captain, or Madam).

To remove a digital ID:

1. Choose Edit/Acrobat > Preferences and choose Security from the list on the left.

2. Click on the ID you want to remove.

3. Click the Delete button. Be sure you want to do this, because you can't undo this action.

✔ Tip

■ You can also edit or duplicate a signature in the Appearance section of the Digital Signature Preferences dialog box.

CREATING A DIGITAL ID

Signing Documents

Now that you have a digital ID, you can sign documents. If a document doesn't already have a signature field, you can create your own and add your signature to it.

To sign a document:

1. Click the Signatures tab on the left side of the document window of the PDF that requires your signature (**Figure 14.9**).

   If the document doesn't already have a signature field, the next step is to create one.

   You can also sign a document using the Sign button in the Tasks toolbar. Choose Sign This Document, then select the Create a New Signature Field to Sign radio button. This combines the creation and the signing steps.

2. Choose Create a Blank Signature Field from the Options menu (**Figure 14.10**).

   A message comes up saying that a signature field has been selected and telling you to click and drag with the mouse to set the area for the signature field (**Figure 14.11**).

3. First click the OK button, then create a Signature box by dragging with your mouse pointer on the document page.

   After you do this, the Digital Signature Properties dialog box appears.

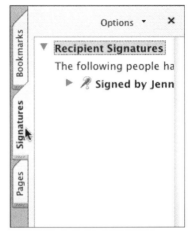

Figure 14.9 The Signatures tab is on the left side of the document window.

Figure 14.10 From the Options menu, choose Create a Blank Signature Field.

Figure 14.11 The message lets you know a signature field was created.

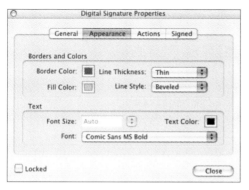

Figure 14.12 You can change the font, text, or border colors.

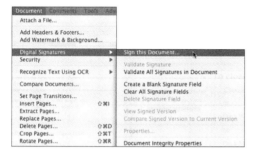

Figure 14.13 The Sign Document dialog box opens when you choose this command.

Figure 14.14 Choose the Sign an Existing Signature Field option.

4. Select the options you want in the Appearance tab, such as border weight, color, and style and fill color for the box. You can also select font and other text options (**Figure 14.12**).

5. Click Close to dismiss the Digital Signature Properties dialog box.

6. Choose Document > Digital Signatures > Sign This Document (**Figure 14.13**).

The Sign Document dialog box opens.

7. Choose Sign an Existing Signature Field (**Figure 14.14**). Click the Next button.

An alert box opens, saying the document has been scrolled and zoomed.

8. Click with the Hand tool on the Digital Signature field to start the process of signing the document. Click the OK button to continue.

The Apply Signature to Document dialog box appears.

(continues on next page)

SIGNING DOCUMENTS

9. Enter your password, choose a reason for signing the document, the Signature Appearance, and any other options you might want in the Options area (**Figure 14.15**).

10. Click Sign and Save (or Sign and Save As).

A note comes up saying you have successfully signed the document (**Figure 14.16**), and your signature appears in the Signatures pane and on the document. Your signature icon or text appears on the PDF (**Figure 14.17**).

Once you have signed your document, you must export your digital ID to a certificate file that holds the information about you as a signer. The next step is to send the certificate file with the signed document to the recipients. Once the recipients receive the file, they must import the certificate file into their copy of Acrobat, thereby adding you to their list of trusted certificates. Now anytime you sign a document for those particular recipients, they can validate your signature.

Figure 14.15 Enter the password and any other options.

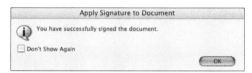

Figure 14.16 Evidence that you have signed the document.

Figure 14.17 The icon appears where you chose to sign the document.

Automating Acrobat

Much of the work involved in creating and editing PDFs and preparing them for distribution is repetitive; you may find yourself opening a series of TIFF files to save as PDFs, or enabling a group of PDFs for commenting in Reader. Also, you may often need to run the same operation on several PDFs at the same time. For instance, you may want to print the first page of every PDF in one folder.

Acrobat's batch processing will let you automate such tasks, relieving you of the tedium. And it will let you combine several commands into a single step, such as removing all file attachments, exporting all images, and embedding page thumbnails.

Using Batch Processing in Acrobat

Batch processing applies a predetermined set of commands, such as opening and printing files, to one or more documents. The best way to process a group of files is to set them up in their own folder and start the batch process before your lunch break or before you leave the office, depending on how many files you are processing.

Acrobat ships with several batch processes; you can customize them or create your own.

◆ **Embed Page Thumbnails** lets you create a permanent set of thumbnails in a document. This can save you time because you won't have to wait for Acrobat to generate thumbnails each time you click the Pages tab (although it does increase file size).

◆ **Fast Web View** allows for more efficient serving of PDF pages from a Web site (also called *byte-serving*). See Chapter 16 for more information.

◆ **Open All** allows you to choose a group of PDFs to open simultaneously.

◆ **Print 1st Page of All** prints the first page of each selected document.

◆ **Print All** executes the Print command for selected documents and prints all pages.

◆ **Remove File Attachments** finds and removes file attachments from PDF documents.

◆ **Save All as RTF** resaves each PDF in Rich Text Format (exports text to a word-processing file).

◆ **Set Security to No Changes** changes the security settings of the selected files to prevent users from changing the documents.

Figure 15.1 Choose Advanced > Batch Processing to start a sequence for one or more files.

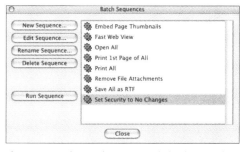

Figure 15.2 In the Batch Sequence dialog box, read the list of default batch sequences.

Figure 15.3 A progress bar shows how much of your sequence has been processed.

To embed page thumbnails:

1. Choose Advanced > Batch Processing (**Figure 15.1**).

   The Batch Sequences dialog box launches (**Figure 15.2**). This dialog box lists the default batch sequences.

2. Select Embed Page Thumbnails in the default list.

3. Click Run Sequence.

   This launches the Run Sequence Confirmation—Embed Page Thumbnails dialog box.

4. Click OK to launch the Select Files to Process dialog box. Choose the files for which you want to embed page thumbnails and then click the Select button.

   A progress bar shows how the process is going for that file (**Figure 15.3**). When the sequence is finished, the file you selected will contain embedded thumbnails.

✔ Tip

■ To select multiple files in which to embed page thumbnails, Shift+click to select multiple contiguous files or Ctrl+click/Command+click to select noncontiguous files.

To batch process all of the files in a folder:

1. Choose Advanced > Batch Processing.

   The Batch Sequences dialog box appears.

2. Select the sequence you want to run, and click the Edit Sequence button.

   The Edit Batch Sequence dialog box appears (**Figure 15.4**).

   You want to process a group of files, so you need to choose a folder in which the batch will be located when you run the process.

3. Choose Selected Folder from the Run Commands On pop-up menu.

4. Click the Choose button.

   The Select Folder to Process dialog box opens (**Figure 15.5**).

5. Select the folder you want to use, and click the Choose button to choose the folder.

6. Back in the Edit Batch Sequence dialog box, choose a location from the Select Output Location pop-up menu.

   This determines where your batch-processed files will end up.

7. Click OK to exit the Edit Batch Sequence dialog box.

   You return to the Batch Sequences dialog box.

8. Choose the sequence you added and click Run Sequence.

   The Run Sequence Confirmation dialog box opens.

9. Click OK to start the batch process.

   A progress bar shows you how the batch sequence is going. The Warnings and Errors section of the Progress dialog box lists any files that aren't PDF files.

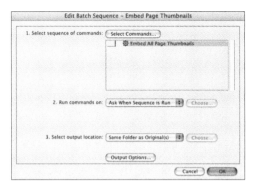

Figure 15.4 The Edit Batch Sequence dialog box opens.

Figure 15.5 The Select Folder to Process dialog box launches.

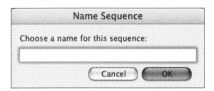

Figure 15.6 The Name Sequence dialog box prompts you to name the sequence.

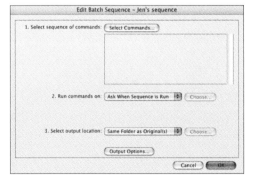

Figure 15.7 In the Edit Batch Sequence dialog box you can add commands.

Creating and Editing Sequences

A batch sequence is nothing more than a list of commands, such as Open and Print, which Acrobat executes one after another when you run the batch process. If you've worked with macros in a word-processing program, or with scripts in desktop publishing or Web design, running sequences won't seem foreign at all. Whether or not you've used these features, creating new sequences and customizing existing ones will be easy.

To create a new batch-processing sequence:

1. Choose Advanced > Batch Processing.
   The Batch Sequences dialog box appears.

2. Click the New Sequence button.
   The Name Sequence dialog box opens (**Figure 15.6**).

3. Enter a descriptive name for the sequence, and click OK.
   The Edit Batch Sequence dialog box opens (**Figure 15.7**).

4. In the Select Sequence of Commands section, click the Select Commands button.
   The Edit Sequence dialog box opens.

(continues on next page)

5. Specify each command that you want Acrobat to perform by selecting the command from the list on the left side of the dialog box and clicking the Add button (**Figure 15.8**).

or

Double-click the command name in the left column to move it to the right column.

The commands appear in the list on the right side of the dialog box.

Some commands have options. For instance, Add Headers & Footers lets you specify the headers and footers.

6. To access the options for a command, select the command from the list on the right, then click the Edit button.

You'll see a new dialog box with a set of controls that you can modify. Click OK to return to the Edit Sequence dialog.

7. To change the order of commands in the right column, select the one you want to move and then click the Move Up or Move Down button.

8. Click OK when you're done choosing commands.

The Edit Sequence dialog box closes, and you return to the Edit Batch Sequence dialog box.

9. In the Run Commands On section, choose the files on which you want your sequence to act from the pop-up menu.

10. If you decided to run commands on a folder, click Choose to open the Select Folder to Process dialog box (**Figure 15.9**), select the folder, and click Choose to return to the Edit Batch Sequence dialog box.

Figure 15.8 Click the Add button to add a command.

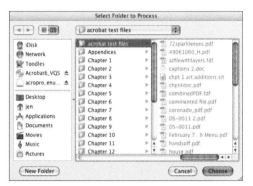

Figure 15.9 You can run a batch sequence on a specified folder.

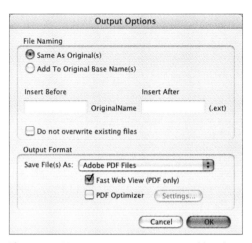

Figure 15.10 You can enter a new name or add to the old one in the Output Options dialog box.

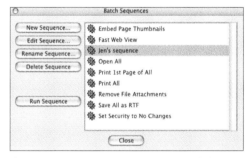

Figure 15.11 Your new sequence is listed with the default sequences.

11. In the Select Output Location section, choose a location from the pop-up menu.

I chose to place output files in the same folder as the originals. If you want to use a different folder, you'll need to click the Choose button to select the folder in which you want to save your files.

12. Click the Output Options button.

The Output Options dialog box opens (**Figure 15.10**).

13. Specify a name to be inserted before or after the original name or to keep the name the same as the original for the processed file.

14. Click OK to set this new sequence. Click OK to return to the Batch Sequence dialog box.

You'll see the new sequence in the Batch Sequences dialog box (**Figure 15.11**).

15. Click the Close button to exit.

If you want to run the batch process you have just created, you need to choose Advanced > Batch Processing and select the new sequence from the list in the Batch Sequences dialog box.

(continues on next page)

CREATING AND EDITING SEQUENCES

✔ Tip

- If you'd like to process types of files other than PDFs (they'll be converted to PDF as part of the operation), click the Source File Options button in the Edit Batch Sequence dialog box (**Figure 15.12**). The Source File Options dialog box opens (**Figure 15.13**), displaying a list of file types you can import.

To edit a batch-processing sequence:

1. Choose Advanced > Batch Processing.

   The Edit Batch Sequence dialog box opens.

2. Choose the sequence you want to edit by selecting it in the list box

3. Click the Edit Sequence button.

   The Edit Batch Sequence dialog box appears.

4. Click Select Commands.

   The Edit Sequence dialog box appears (**Figure 15.14**).

5. Add or remove commands to change the batch sequence; then click OK.

   The Edit Sequence dialog box closes, and you return to the Edit Batch Sequences dialog box.

6. Click OK to exit the Edit Batch Sequence dialog box.

7. Click the Close button to exit the Batch Sequences dialog box.

   Now the sequence you edited is ready to perform batch processing.

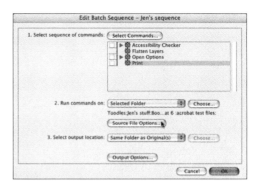

Figure 15.12 Click the Source File Options button to proceed.

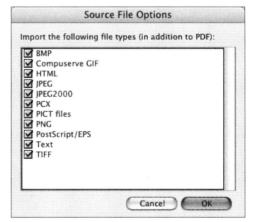

Figure 15.13 The Source File Options dialog box shows you a list of files you can import.

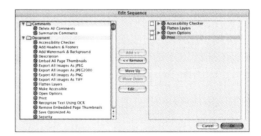

Figure 15.14 The Edit Sequence dialog box opens.

Figure 15.15 Choose Batch Processing from the list on the left in the Preferences dialog box.

Setting Batch Preferences

Acrobat doesn't offer many batch-processing options, but the ones it does have can be helpful in streamlining your work processes, especially depending on which Security Handler option (no security, password security, certificate security, or Adobe Policy Server) you set.

To set batch preferences:

1. Choose Edit/Acrobat > Preferences.

2. Choose Batch Processing from the list on the left (**Figure 15.15**).

   You see the Batch Processing options:

   ▲ **Show the Run Sequence Confirmation Dialog** shows you the progress of the batch processing whenever you run a batch process.

   ▲ **Save Warnings and Errors in Log File** saves a record of all the warnings and errors that come up when you're running a batch process.

   ▲ **Security Method** determines what Acrobat does when it encounters a document that requires a password. If this option is set to Do Not Ask for Password, batch processing stops when Acrobat encounters a document with password protection. Therefore, it's a good idea to set uniform password security so you can run the sequence without stopping.

3. Make any changes, and click OK.

✔ Tip

■ If you're planning to run a sequence on documents that are password protected, make sure that all the documents in your directory have the same password. Otherwise, only the documents with the password you enter at the beginning of the sequence run will actually be processed.

PDF FILES AND THE WEB

16

The World Wide Web has transformed the world into an HTML-based society of Internet junkies. It wouldn't be too bad if HTML were compact, and flexible, and produced good-looking content, but that's not always the case. Professional Web designers and amateurs alike know that browser differences can distort the most carefully designed page. Add the unpredictability of Web viewers' monitor settings, and you have a desperate need for a stable, dependable format for documents: hence, PDF.

PDFs are everywhere on the Internet: as eBooks, order forms on retail sites, help files, and even downloadable tax forms. When the IRS adopts your technology, you know you've arrived.

This chapter discusses how to use Acrobat and PDF files on the Web, from reading pages online to creating and displaying them on your own Web server.

Reading PDF Pages Online

PDF files can be viewed live on the Internet by a variety of browsers. If the Web server hosting the pages is configured properly, and the PDFs themselves are optimized, the pages are sent one at a time so a reader who wants to view only pages 1, 3, 16, and 243 doesn't have to download the entire 300-page document. Normally, the Acrobat Installer configures your Web browser to read PDFs online, but this section shows you how to set up your browser manually so that you can customize it. These are the options you set in Acrobat Preferences when you choose Internet from the list on the left of the Preferences window:

◆ **Display PDF in Browser Using** will let you view PDFs in your Web browser. If this option isn't checked, your browser will launch Acrobat and display the PDF.

◆ **Check Browser Settings when Starting Acrobat** checks for application compatibility. Some of the less mainstream browser applications, as well as some older browsers, cannot be configured to launch PDF files.

◆ **Allow Fast Web View** will display one page at a time rather than waiting until the whole document is downloaded.

◆ **Allow Speculative Downloading in the Background** tells Acrobat to try to figure out what page you want to view next and download it in the background. This process will stop if you attempt a different function in Acrobat, so you can choose this option without slowing down Acrobat's performance.

◆ **Connection Speed** allows you to specify your Internet connection speed.

◆ **Network Settings** enables you to set up your Internet connection and input information such as your service provider, type of modem, and account information.

Figure 16.1 Make sure that the Display PDF in Browser option is selected.

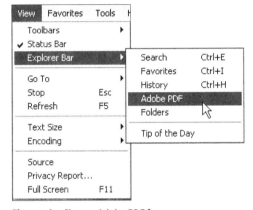

Figure 16.2 Choose Adobe PDF from the Explorer Bar submenu.

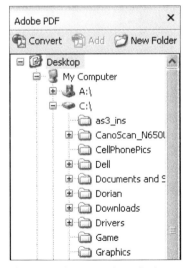

Figure 16.3 The PDF Explorer displays your computer and its contents for easy browsing.

To set up your Web browser to read PDF files

1. Choose File/Acrobat > Preferences (Ctrl+K/Command+K).

   Choose Internet from the list on the left.

2. Make sure Display PDF in Browser Using is checked (**Figure 16.1**) and that Adobe Acrobat 7.0 Professional shows in the pop up menu.

   If you don't have this option checked the PDF will open directly into Acrobat, rather than launching Acrobat via your Web browser.

3. Change any other settings as necessary (see the list of options described earlier), and click OK.

To view a test PDF document in Explorer (Windows):

1. Launch your Web browser.

2. Choose View > Explorer Bar > Adobe PDF (**Figure 16.2**).

   This lets you navigate your computer in the left pane and choose a PDF file to open, convert a Web page to a PDF, add a Web page to an existing PDF, print a Web page, or convert a Web page and email it (**Figure 16.3**).

3. Find the PDF you want to open in your browser and double-click the filename.

   The PDF page appears in your Web browser.

✔ Tips

- Acrobat will load as an application in the background, so you'll need enough free RAM to run your browser and the Acrobat application at the same time.

- Most PDF files have the extension .pdf. In fact, if they don't, your Web browser won't recognize them as PDFs.

Editing PDFs Online

You can edit PDFs within a Web browser, just as you would with Acrobat. This is especially useful when you're collaborating on work, because several people can add comments to the same document, and see one anothers' comments as well.

Be aware, however, that you can't edit just any old PDF that your browser displays. The PDF must be hosted on a server that's properly configured, which is beyond the scope of this book. Consult your network administrator if you need to set up PDFs for online editing, and refer to Chapters 7, 8, and 9 for more on commenting and reviewing.

EDITING PDFs ONLINE

Linking a Web Page to a PDF

Although you can't actually embed a PDF file in a Web page the way you do a graphic file, you can set a link that readers can click on to display the document.

To link to a PDF:

1. Working in your HTML document, choose a spot for the link.

2. In your HTML editor, type the following line:

   `<A HREF="pdfs/MyPage.pdf">Click here to read my PDF</A>`**pdfs** should refer to the folder containing your Acrobat documents, which must reside in the same folder as your HTML file. **MyPage.pdf** should be the name of your document. **"Click here to read my PDF"** is the text of the link itself.

3. Save the HTML document.

4. Open the document in a Web browser.

5. Click the link.

   The PDF file displays in your browser window.

   Any HTML link to a PDF file will display the PDF file in the browser's window. So, you don't need to manually code your link. Just link to a PDF in an application such as Macromedia Dreamweaver and it will behave exactly like the hand-coded link described above.

Distributing Acrobat Reader on the Web

When you purchase Acrobat, you'll also get a CD with Acrobat Reader on it. Acrobat Reader is available for free downloading and distribution. First read Adobe's licensing agreement to ensure that you are distributing Reader properly. You must register with Adobe to be a Reader distributor. Go to www.adobe.com:80/products/acrobat/distribute.html, and read the steps you must take. Fill out the online form at Adobe's Web site at www.adobe.com:80/products/acrobat/acrrdistribute.html. In addition, be sure to get the logos for creating the links from your site to Adobe's site by following the steps outlined by Adobe.

You can also provide a link to the Adobe Acrobat Reader Web page, from which visitors can download the latest version of Reader.

Optimizing PDF Files for Online Viewing

When a Web server delivers a PDF one page at a time, it's called byte-serving. In order for byte-serving to work, the PDF files must first be optimized. You can set optimization as the default behavior, although in Acrobat 5 or earlier you have to select optimization as an option at the time you save a file. Byte-serving is a function of the server hosting the PDF files, not a function of Acrobat. The following task shows you how to prepare a PDF file for a server on which byte-serving is enabled.

Figure 16.4 You must check the Save As Optimizes for Fast Web View option to allow users to download your PDF one page at a time.

To optimize PDF files for byte-serving:

1. Choose Edit/Acrobat > Preferences to open Acrobat Preferences.

2. In the list on the left side of the window, select General.

3. Make sure that the Save As Optimizes for Fast Web View option is checked (**Figure 16.4**).

4. Click OK.

   Any file you save should now be optimized, and can be sent to the browser one page at a time.

   It's important to note, however, that optimization is not guaranteed when you save a modified PDF file. You must select File > Save As and save the file with a different name.

✔ Tip

- Your Web administrator can probably tell you whether your Web site is set up to byte-serve PDF files. If not, explain that you'd like to byte-serve PDF files, and the administrator will probably be able to upgrade the server software or direct you to a Web server that can byte-serve.

Removing Optimization from PDF Files

In some cases, you may want viewers to download an entire document at the same time instead of page by page. If viewers have an entire document on their systems, they'll be able to access individual pages much faster than if the pages have to be downloaded individually. To provide this capability, you must create nonoptimized files.

To remove optimization from PDF files:

1. Choose Edit/Acrobat > Preferences (Ctrl+K/Command+K).
   The Preferences dialog box appears.

2. In the list on the left side of the dialog box, select General.

3. Uncheck the Save As Optimizes for Fast Web View check box.

4. Click OK.

5. Open the PDF file.

6. Choose Save As from the File menu.
   The Save As dialog box appears.

7. Click the Save button.
   Now the file will be downloaded in its entirety when it is viewed with a Web browser.

Acrobat Help

Figure A.1 The Windows Help menu.

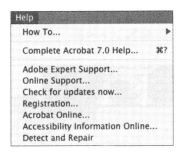

Figure A.2 The Macintosh Help menu.

As much as you like to think you know a program, you may occasionally need help. Acrobat has a few features that provide you with all the help you're likely to need. The main feature is the Help menu, which will help you troubleshoot problems and find the right tools (**Figures A.1** and **A.2**).

If it's not an answer to a particular question that you're looking for but you would like to take a tutorial on specific tasks in Acrobat, you can turn to Acrobat's How To feature. It takes you step by step through such tasks as

◆ Commenting on and marking up your PDFs

◆ Creating PDFs

◆ Securing your document

◆ Signing your document and more.

Exploring the Help Menu

To access Help, choose Complete Acrobat 7.0 Help from the Help menu (F1/Command+?). When Adobe Acrobat Help opens, it displays tabs for the three main sections of the file: Contents, Search, and Index (**Figure A.3**). Each tab gives you access to the same topics; which one you use depends on your preferred working style.

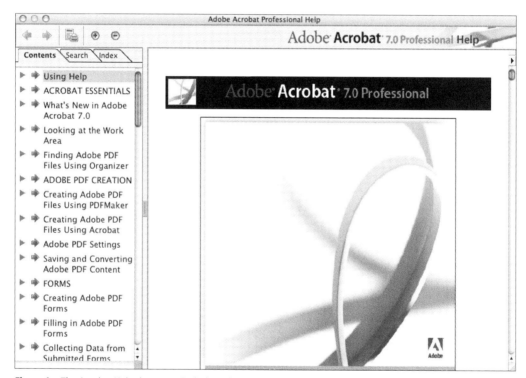

Figure A.3 The Acrobat Help document includes tabs for the main sections.

EXPLORING THE HELP MENU

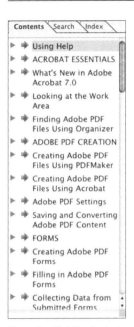

Figure A.4 Click the Contents tab in the Help pane.

Using Contents

Each topic in the Help file is bookmarked so that you can jump to it quickly. To help you find specific items, bookmarks are grouped hierarchically in the Help pane.

To use Contents:

1. Click the Contents tab at the top of the Help pane (**Figure A.4**).

   You see a list of main topics in the Help file, with links to each topic.

2. Click the triangle to the left of a bookmark to display the list of chapters in the Contents pane (**Figure A.5**).

   Each chapter has its own triangle, indicating further levels exist deeper in the hierarchy.

(continues on next page)

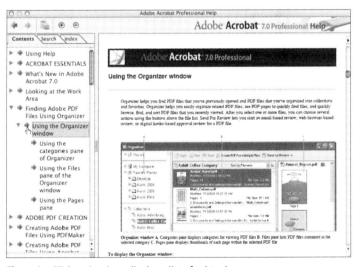

Figure A.5 Click a triangle to display a list of subtopics.

3. Click the topic in the Contents pane that you want to view (**Figure A.6**).

Acrobat displays the page for that topic in the Document pane (**Figure A.7**).

Acrobat provides a back button, which takes you to the last page you viewed (**Figure A.8**), and an option to print the topic as well as to zoom in or out of the topic pane.

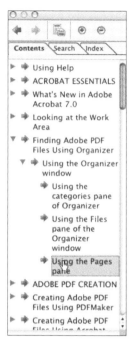

Figure A.6 Click the topic you want to view.

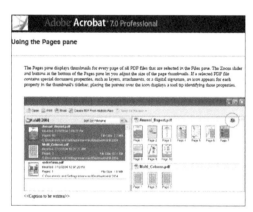

Figure A.7 Acrobat displays the page for that topic.

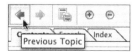

Figure A.8 If you want to go back a page you most recently viewed, press this button.

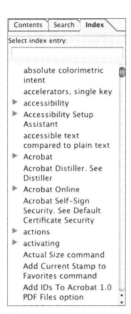

Figure A.9 Enter a topic in the Select Index Entry field.

Using the Index

The Index is my favorite way to find information on a subject in Acrobat. It's quicker than scrolling through a table of contents or using the Search tab.

To search with the Index:

1. Click the Index tab.

   An alphabetic listing of the topics appears in the Index pane, with arrows indicating nested topics (**Figure A.9**).

2. Enter the topic you want to look for in the Select Index Entry field.

3. When you find the topic, click it to go to that page in the Help document.

USING THE INDEX

Using Search

You can type a word or words in the Search tab of Help to find a specific topic. Search is handy if you already know the exact wording of the Help topics or the general thread, such as PDF or Printing, but for more obscure topics, you're better off using the Index.

To use Search:

1. In the Help pane, click the Search tab.

2. In the text box, enter the topic you wish to find Help on.

   I typed **Printing** for this example.

3. Click the Search button (**Figure A.10**). The search results are listed on the left pane.

4. Click the topic you wish to view and it shows up in the Help pane, with the search term highlighted (**Figure A.11**).

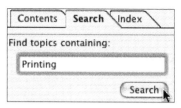

Figure A.10 Click the Search button to find your topic.

Figure A.11 The topic you chose shows up in the Help pane.

Printing Help Topics

You can print any of the topics you're reading for future reference.

To print Help topics:

1. Select the topic you want to print.

2. Click the Print Topic button at the top of the left-hand window.

   The Print dialog box appears (**Figure A.12**), with the appropriate page numbers already filled in.

3. Click the Print button to print the topic.

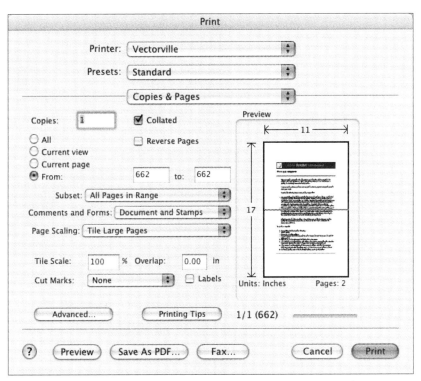

Figure A.12 Type the desired page numbers in the text boxes, and click the Print button.

Using Other Help Menu Items

The Help menu includes other items to assist you with Acrobat. Although one could argue that these aren't help in the strictest sense, it's undeniable that one-click connections to information, updates, and online registration are wonderful features.

◆ **Adobe Expert Support** opens up the Adobe Expert Support Web page (**Figure A.13**), where you can sign up and purchase a year's worth of technical support from Adobe's support experts.

◆ **Online Support** takes you to the free online support Web page (**Figure A.14**), where you can check for errors, troubleshoot problems for Acrobat, and link to the top Help issues.

◆ **Check for Updates Now** instructs Acrobat to look online for any updates to the Acrobat 7.0 Professional application.

◆ **Registration** lets you register your copy of Acrobat instantly. Acrobat starts your Web browser and takes you to the registration page on Adobe's Web site (**Figure A.15**).

Figure A.13 Choosing Adobe Expert Support lets you opt to purchase technical online help from Adobe.

Figure A.14 Choosing Online Support takes you to Adobe's online support Web page.

Figure A.15 You can register your copy of Acrobat online.

Figure A.16 Acrobat provides a one-click connection to customer support.

Figure A.17 Check to see what Accessibility features Acrobat offers.

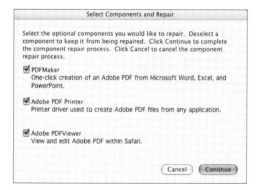

Figure A.18 Detect and Repair keeps Acrobat running smoothly.

◆ **Acrobat Online** takes you directly to Adobe's Acrobat home page (**Figure A.16**). From there, choose any of the topics you want to know more about.

◆ **Accessibility Information Online** takes you directly to Adobe's Accessibility home page (**Figure A.17**). Select any of the topics you want to learn more about.

◆ **Detect and Repair** looks for any missing components of the Acrobat 7 Professional application. When you choose Detect and Repair, the Select Components and Repair dialog box opens (**Figure A.18**). Choose the components you are having trouble with (PDFMaker, Adobe PDF Printer, or Adobe PDFViewer) and click the Continue button. If Detect and Repair finds missing components, it will repair them and open an alert box.

These additional items are offered in the Windows Help menu. On Macintosh, these items are found under the Acrobat menu.

◆ **About Acrobat 7.0** displays the Acrobat splash screen, which lists the team that created Acrobat, the release version, the person to whom the copy is licensed, and the serial number. Click anywhere on the splash screen to close it.

◆ **About Adobe Plug-Ins** opens the About Adobe Plug-Ins dialog box, which lists all the standard Acrobat plug-ins. Select a plug-in from the list on the left, and Acrobat displays information on it on the right side of the dialog box. Click OK to exit.

USING OTHER HELP MENU ITEMS

◆ **About Third-Party Plug-Ins** lets you get information about any third-party plug-ins that you have installed (**Figure A.19**).

◆ **System Info** displays information about your computer (**Figure A.20**). (On Macs, click About This Mac under the Apple menu to get this type of information.) You can send a report about your system information to your IT person, for example, by clicking Send Report. This launches your email program with your system information attached.

✔ Tip

■ You can find a list of Adobe-approved third-party plug-ins at Adobe's Web site (www.adobe.com/products/plugins/ acrobat/main.html).

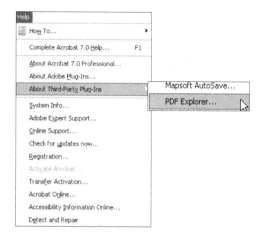

Figure A.19 Here's where to start if you need information about your third-party plug-ins.

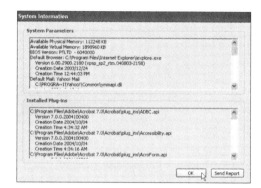

Figure A.20 This box displays the Macintosh's system information.

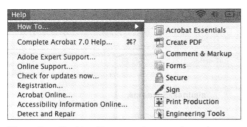

Figure A.21 The How To pane takes you through a variety of tasks.

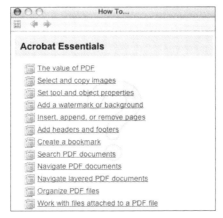

Figure A.22 Acrobat Essentials tackles the crucial tasks.

Figure A.23 One of the main topics is Create PDF.

Using the How To Area

The How To area provides a great way to go through various tasks that Acrobat has to offer. Choose a topic, and this wonderful feature explains step by step how to do it. If the How To pane on the right of the document window is not visible, choose Help > How To > *any topic*. The pane lists the basic topics: Acrobat Essentials, Create PDF, Comment & Markup, Forms, Secure, Sign, Print Production, and Engineering Tools (**Figure A.21**).

◆ **Acrobat Essentials** lists topics that cover some of the more important features, such as adding a bookmark, navigation, and organizing (**Figure A.22**).

◆ **Create PDF** brings up a list of subtopics (**Figure A.23**). The subtopics cover the various ways to create PDFs, including from a file, from a Web site, from a scanned document, and from Microsoft Office, Autodesk's AutoCad, or other applications.

◆ **Comment & Markup** takes you through the commenting, review, and marking up process (**Figure A.24**), from setting up a review to editing text and dealing with comments.

◆ **Forms** explains how to fill in an interactive form in Acrobat (**Figure A.25**).

◆ **Secure** covers how to create a certified document, add a document password, restrict printing or changes to a document, create security policies (so you can reuse the security settings), and create eEnvelopes (an encrypted file attachment for secure file sending) (**Figure A.26**).

◆ **Sign** explains how to set up a digital ID, create a blank signature field, sign a document, change a signature appearance, share certificate information, get another user's certificate information, and validate signatures.

◆ **Print Production** covers using preflight, previewing color separations, printing color separations, previewing transparency flattening, and creating a PDF/X-compliant file (the standards set for fonts, colors, bounding boxes, etc. that create printing issues).

◆ **Engineering Tools** walks you through using advanced zoom tools, navigating a layered PDF, measuring, using scaling and rulers, viewing split screens, customizing viewing, and viewing object metadata (information on an image that lets you access the image, such as the digital representation, security, and more).

Figure A.24 Learn how to add comments and mark up your PDF.

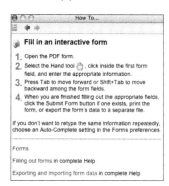

Figure A.25 Add information in an interactive PDF form.

Figure A.26 Learn how to secure your PDF.

DOCUMENT SECURITY

B

Are you concerned that your document may fall into the wrong hands or that readers may try to change your prose? Or maybe you'd like to distribute your document electronically but don't want that document to be printed and possibly distributed to unauthorized users.

Acrobat's built-in security options can prevent unauthorized access, printing, and editing of your PDF files. Secured PDF files stand up to rigorous attempts to bypass their password-protection schemes.

Adding Security to a PDF

By default, PDF documents are open, meaning that anyone can open the file, make changes, resave it, copy text and images from it, and work with the file as his or her own. You can add security options to a PDF document manually or as part of a batch sequence (see Chapter 15). A PDF file can have two types of password security: one for opening the file, and one for altering or copying its contents.

To add password security to a PDF:

1. Open the document you want to add a password to.

2. Choose File > Document Properties and click the Security tab in the resulting Document Properties dialog box.

3. Select Password Security from the Security Method pop-up menu (**Figure B.1**).

   This launches the Password Security – Settings dialog box (**Figure B.2**).

Figure B.1 Open the Password Security pop-up menu and choose Password Security.

Figure B.2 The Password Security – Settings dialog box lets you apply security settings to your PDF.

Figure B.3 Specify whether you want to allow printing or changes to your PDF.

Figure B.4 Reenter your password.

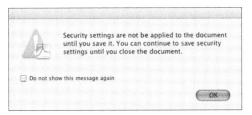

Figure B.5 The warning box alerts you that you need to save and close the document.

✔ **Tip**

■ Acrobat has no limit on the length of a password, but the password is case-sensitive.

4. Select the appropriate setting from the Compatibility pop-up menu.

5. To activate a password for opening a file, click the Require a Password to Open the Document check box, then enter a password.

6. If you'd like to enter a password that restricts printing and editing of the document, click the first check box in the Permissions section of the dialog box and enter a password. Then, choose whether to allow printing or changes from the pop-up menus.

I chose to allow low-resolution printing but no editing for this PDF document (**Figure B.3**).

7. Click the OK button, and the Acrobat Security dialog box opens. You'll need to enter the Document Open Password again to confirm the password. Enter the password, and click OK (**Figure B.4**).

A warning dialog box appears letting you know that Adobe products enforce restrictions set by the permissions password but that third-party recipients may be able to bypass your restrictions.

8. Click OK.

Since I set a password for permissions as well, the Adobe Acrobat – Confirm Permissions Password dialog box opens.

9. Reenter the Permissions Password and click OK.

A warning box comes up (**Figure B.5**) alerting you that security settings will not be applied until the document has been saved and closed.

10. Click OK.

At this point, the document is locked. The only way to reopen it is to supply the password.

ADDING SECURITY TO A PDF

To remove security from a document:

1. Open the document, using the password.

2. Choose File > Document Properties.
The Document Properties dialog box appears.

3. Click the Security tab.

4. Choose No Security from the Security Method pop-up menu.
The resulting dialog box asks you for the password.

5. Type the password and click OK.
Now the document can be opened without a password.

Other standard security options

Besides allowing you to prevent a document from being opened without a password, Acrobat provides several other types of protection.

When setting the permissions for printing and changes, you have a few other choices. Under the Printing Allowed pop-up menu, you can choose from high resolution or low resolution. The Changes Allowed pop-up menu offers these options:

◆ **None** means that no one can make any changes to your PDF.

◆ **Inserting, Deleting, and Rotating Pages** lets the user insert, delete, and rotate any pages in the PDF.

◆ **Filling In Form Fields and Signing** is the best option when you're sending forms because it allows the user to fill in the form and sign the document.

◆ **Commenting, Filling In Form Fields, and Signing** lets the user comment on the file, fill in the form fields, and sign the PDF.

◆ **Any Except Extracting Pages** enables the user to do anything to the PDF except remove or extract pages.

Choosing a Password

If keeping your document secure is important, the most important thing you can do is choose a good password. Keep the following rules in mind:

◆ Don't pick an easy-to-guess password, such as the name of a child, friend, pet, or spouse. If someone you know can guess your password, it's too easy.

◆ Combine numerals and letters. If you use only numbers in an 8-character password, 10 million combinations are possible. If you use a combination of 8 letters and numbers, the combinations total almost 3 trillion.

◆ Make your password easy to remember but hard to guess.

ADDING SECURITY TO A PDF

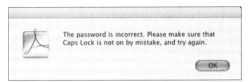

Figure B.6 If you see this dialog box, you know the document is password protected.

Figure B.7 An alert lets you know that you entered the wrong password.

Opening Secure PDFs

Opening a password-protected document, whether it's one that you protected or one you received from someone else, takes only a moment.

To open a locked PDF file:

1. Double-click the file's icon or select it in Acrobat's Open dialog box.

   The Password dialog box appears, notifying you that the document is protected by a password (**Figure B.6**) and asking you to enter the password.

2. Enter the password and click OK to open the document.

   If you enter the correct password, the document opens.

   If you enter the wrong password, an alert box appears (**Figure B.7**). Click OK to return to the Password dialog box; then enter the correct password and click OK.

✔ Tip

■ After three unsuccessful attempts at entering the correct password, the dialog box ceases to appear, and you must open the document again by double-clicking its icon or using Acrobat's Open dialog box.

Checking Security Settings

After you open a locked document, you can check the security settings that the author of the document specified for the file. These settings let you know what you're free to do with the file.

To check the security settings of a file:

1. Open the document for which you want to check security.

2. Choose Document Properties from the File menu.

   The Document Properties dialog box appears.

3. Click the Show Details button to display the security settings for the open document (**Figure B.8**).

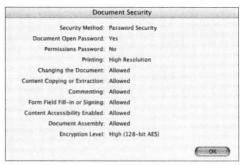

Figure B.8 The Document Security window shows in what ways you're allowed to alter a document.

ACCESSIBILITY

Acrobat's accessibility features enable anyone with motor and vision challenges to use PDF files with relative ease. For example, you can have Acrobat read text out loud, or you can control the magnification at which the PDF opens. The areas that accessibility covers are speech, visibility, navigation, and the keyboard.

Reading Out Loud

Part of Adobe's efforts to accommodate visually impaired users, the Read Out Loud command will read a page or a whole document out loud. The Read Aloud feature converts text to spoken words. You can choose to have one page read or the whole document, and you can specify the reading order. While a PDF is being read out loud, you can always pause or stop the reading.

To have a PDF file read out loud:

1. Choose View > Read Out Loud and either Read This Page Only or Read to End of Document (**Figure C.1**). You can also press Ctrl+Shift+V/Command+Shift+V for the current page or Ctrl+Shift+B/Command+Shift+B to read to the end of the document.

   The default voice will start reading.

2. To pause the reading, choose View > Read Out Loud > Pause (**Figure C.2**).

   The reading will pause. You can also press Ctrl+Shift+C/Command+Shift+C to pause; press it again to continue reading.

3. To stop the reading, choose View > Read Out Loud > Stop, or press Ctrl+Shift+E/Command+Shift+E.

Figure C.1 Acrobat can read a PDF document out loud to you.

Figure C.2 You can pause while Acrobat is reading to you.

Setting Reading Options

Choose from a variety of voices under the Reading preferences. To access the Reading preferences, open the Preferences dialog box, then choose Reading from the list of topics on the left. Choose a voice, pitch, and words per minute. You can also set the reading order and screen reader options.

To set the Reading options:

1. Choose File/Acrobat > Preferences.

2. Choose Reading from the list on the left. This displays the default reading preference settings (**Figure C.3**).

3. Set the desired volume level.

(continues on next page)

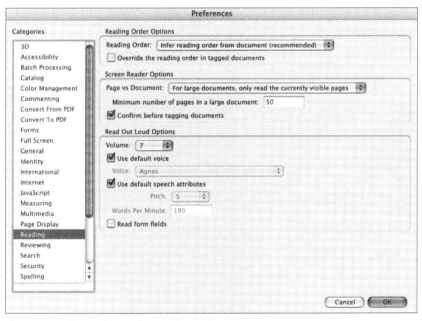

Figure C.3 Set the Reading preferences for Acrobat.

4. Choose a voice.

On Windows you have only the default voice. The Macintosh lets you choose from among a variety of voices. Keep in mind that some voices sound better than others. You can set the pitch and words per minute on both Mac and Windows.

5. Choose a reading order from the pop-up menu (**Figure C.4**):

▲ **Infer Reading Order from Document** is generally the best method for reading a document. This option reads in the order that the document is tagged. If the document isn't tagged, it will use the most logical reading order.

▲ **Left-to-Right, Top-to-Bottom Reading Order** will read the PDF strictly from left to right and top to bottom, regardless of how the document was created.

▲ **Use Reading Order in Raw Print Stream** reads the words in the order they were recorded.

6. Click OK.

Some of the other options you can set are the Screen Reader Options. In this section you can set the Page vs. Document pop-up menu to read only the currently visible pages or to read the entire document.

You can also set the volume, voice, pitch, and words read per minute. If you are reading a form, check the Read Form Fields box so that Acrobat will read all of the form fields as well.

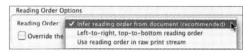

Figure C.4 Choose a reading order for your PDF document.

SETTING READING OPTIONS

Figure C.5 Change the default zoom for your PDF in the Page Display panel of Preferences.

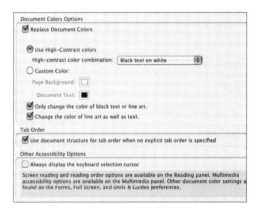

Figure C.6 Change the Document Colors Options for better visibility in the Accessibility panel of Preferences.

Other Accessibility Options

There are a number of other simple things you can do to make your document more accessible to all readers. You'll find some of these features in Preferences and some in other areas of the program.

Visibility

One of the quickest ways to make your PDF more readable for people with vision challenges is to change its viewing methods. You can change the Default Zoom in the Magnification section of the Page Display panel of Preferences (**Figure C.5**). For more on setting these preferences, see Chapter 2.

In the Accessibility panel of Preferences, you'll find other options that increase the visibility of text and graphics on your pages, such as changing the Document Colors Options (**Figure C.6**). For example, you can choose to replace the page background and text colors so that the text is more visible to the reader.

Automatic scrolling

Using the Automatic Scrolling feature lets you move through a PDF without relying on the mouse.

To scroll automatically:

1. With the document open, choose View > Automatically Scroll (**Figure C.7**) or press Ctrl+Shift+H/Command+Shift+H. The document will start scrolling slowly down your screen.

2. Use the number keys to control the speed of the scrolling, with 9 being fastest and 0 being slowest.

3. Use the up and down arrow keys to change the direction of scrolling. You can also use the hyphen or minus key to go backward.

4. To go to the previous or next page, use the left or right arrows. To stop scrolling at any time, press Ctrl+Shift+H/Command+Shift+H (which turns on or off Automatic Scrolling).

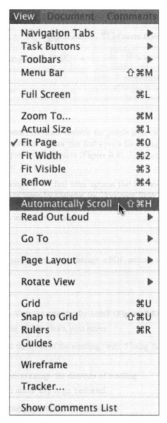

Figure C.7 You can choose to have your PDF scroll automatically.

OTHER ACCESSIBILITY OPTIONS

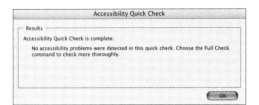

Figure C.8 Run a Quick Check on your PDF for accessibility.

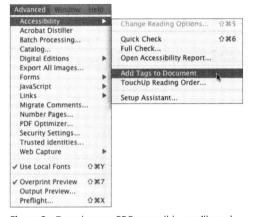

Figure C.9 To make your PDF accessible, you'll need to add tags to your document.

Page Pass: page 7 of 8; Evaluate Knowledge Source

Figure C.10 You'll see the progress of the tags at the bottom of your PDF document window.

Checking the Accessibility of Your PDF

You can check how accessible your PDF is. Acrobat runs a check on the structure and tags of the PDF to make sure the document can be made accessible. It also checks for protection settings and for images that are scanned (in other words, they are not accessible).

To check for accessibility:

◆ Choose Advanced > Accessibility > Quick Check.

A window appears, containing a brief report on the accessibility of your document (**Figure C.8**).

If you want to see a report detailing the accessibility problems, choose the Full Check option under the Accessibility submenu. This will allow you to generate a viewable report of the issues found in the PDF document. For more on running a Full Check for an accessibility report, see the next section, "Creating an Accessibility Report."

To check your PDF for accessibility problems:

1. Open the PDF you want to make accessible.

2. Choose Advanced > Accessibility > Add Tags to Document (**Figure C.9**).

   Tags indicate the reading order of the PDF document. They direct the Read Out Loud feature to follow the reading order specified with the document.

   A progress bar appears at the bottom of the document page (**Figure C.10**). When it's completed, you can view an Add Tags Report if any problems occurred.

   Your document won't look any different: The tagged areas are hidden in the background.

CHECKING THE ACCESSIBILITY OF YOUR PDF

Creating an Accessibility Report

To view an actual report of any accessibility problems, you'll need to run a Full Check on your PDF document. The report will help you avoid the same problems when you create other PDF documents for accessibility. The report will show you what the problems are and how to fix them for this document as well as others.

To create an accessibility report:

1. Open the PDF you want to make accessible.

2. Choose Advanced > Accessibility > Full Check (**Figure C.11**).

   The Accessibility Full Check dialog box opens.

3. In the Accessibility Full Check dialog box, check the Create Accessibility Report box and then click the Browse button to find a location on your hard drive to save the report (**Figure C.12**). Include any other options you want for running Full Check, such as the page range, text language, form field descriptions, and more.

4. Click the Start Checking button to start the process.

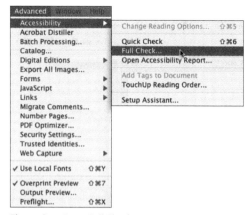

Figure C. 11 Run a Full Check on your PDF to create an accessibility report.

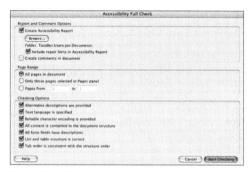

Figure C.12 Click Browse to choose a location on your computer to save your report.

CREATING AN ACCESSIBILITY REPORT

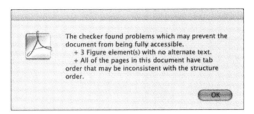

Figure C.13 A warning box displays problems with the file.

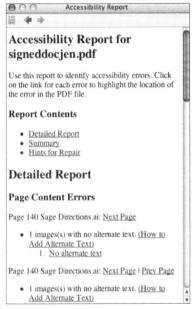

Figure C.14 Acrobat displays this report to help you identify and repair accessibility errors.

5. A warning dialog box will list the problems with the PDF file (**Figure C.13**). Click OK and the Accessibility Report will launch (**Figure C.14**). If you want to view the report at any time, choose Advanced > Accessibility > Open Accessibility Report. Locate the report, which will be stored where you specified in step 3.

✔ Tip

- A Full Check can take quite a bit of time. To stop the Full Check, press the Esc key. You can set a smaller page range for the report in the Full Check dialog box.

TouchUp Reading Order

You can use the TouchUp Reading tool to change the reading order of a PDF document. The tool is relatively easy to use. You drag a rectangle around the area you want to change and choose the type of text in the TouchUp Reading Order dialog box. To adjust the Reading order, the PDF document must first be tagged. For more on tagging your document, see the previous section.

To TouchUp the Reading order of a PDF:

1. Open the PDF for which you want to specify a different reading order.

2. Choose Advanced > Accessibility > TouchUp Reading Order.

   The TouchUp Reading Order dialog box opens (**Figure C.15**).

3. Draw a rectangle around the content you want to change, then click one of the buttons in the dialog box. This sets the tag for the selection, for example, you could select text and define it by clicking the Text button. In the Order pane (which you access by choosing View > Navigation Tabs > Order), you can change the order in which the document is read simply by dragging pages to rearrange their order (**Figure C.16**).

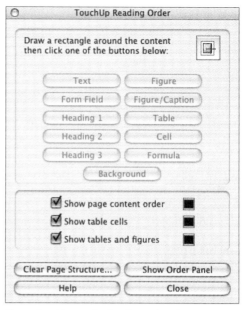

Figure C.15 Change the Reading order of your PDF in the TouchUp Reading Order dialog box.

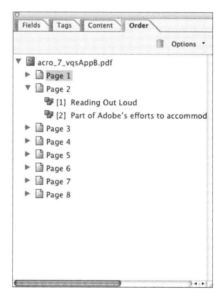

Figure C.16 The Order pane lets you change the reading order of the pages.

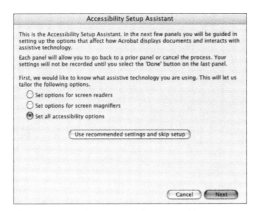

Figure C.17 Use the Setup Assistant to add accessibility to your PDF.

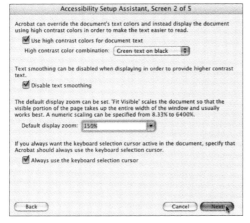

Figure C.18 Set the visual display of the PDF in this screen.

Using the Setup Assistant

The Setup Assistant is a wizard that enables you to go through a procedure step by step, making a document accessible for readers. Choose from three options: Set Options for Screen Readers, Set Options for Screen Magnifiers, or Set All Accessibility Options. Alternatively, you can choose the option Use Recommended Settings and Skip the Setup.

To use the Setup Assistant to set all accessibility options:

1. Open the PDF you want to make accessible.

2. Choose Advanced > Accessibility > Setup Assistant.

   The Accessibility Setup Assistant dialog box opens (**Figure C.17**).

3. Choose the Set All Accessibility Options radio button; then click the Next button.

4. In Screen 2 of 5, set the contrast colors, text smoothing, default display zoom, and the keyboard selection cursor; then click the Next button (**Figure C.18**).

   (continues on next page)

USING THE SETUP ASSISTANT

5. In Screen 3 of 5, set the reading order, overrides, and confirmation of tags; then click the Next button.

6. In Screen 4 of 5, set the accessing of pages and the maximum number of pages. Click the Next button.

7. In Screen 5 of 5, set the autosave, reopen, and display options. Then click the Done button to finish the process of making your PDF accessible.

The PDF is displayed with your chosen accessibility features (**Figure C.19**).

Figure C.19 The altered PDF will display your changes to make it more accessible.

USING THE SETUP ASSISTANT

INDEX

Index

Index

Index

BOOKS ONLINE

ENABLED

THIS BOOK IS SAFARI ENABLED

INCLUDES FREE 45-DAY ACCESS TO THE ONLINE EDITION

The Safari® Enabled icon on the cover of your favorite technology book means the book is available through Safari Bookshelf. When you buy this book, you get free access to the online edition for 45 days.

Safari Bookshelf is an electronic reference library that lets you easily search thousands of technical books, find code samples, download chapters, and access technical information whenever and wherever you need it.

TO GAIN 45-DAY SAFARI ENABLED ACCESS TO THIS BOOK:

- Go to **http://www.peachpit.com/safarienabled**

- Complete the brief registration form

- Enter the coupon code found in the front of this book before the Table of Contents

If you have difficulty registering on Safari Bookshelf or accessing the online edition, please e-mail customer-service@safaribooksonline.com.